Our men must become more earn
are essential in building vibrant, he
captured with clear insight, the ne
life and onto their personal, God-giv

for every disciple.

—Dr. Gary Benedict
Past president, Christian and Missionary Alliance

Les Tripp's passion for discipling men comes through loud and clear. His energy and experience in leading men are apparent as he draws out the principles of success and failure from the life of Joshua. This is excellent material and a wonderful contribution to ministry to men. It is clear, practical, and to the point. It is useful for personal study, small groups, and mentoring.

—Dr. Randy Corbin
Former superintendent, Mid-Atlantic District of the
Christian and Christian Missionary Alliance

The evidence is clear and compelling. In many churches there is a strong desire to talk about radical discipleship, but a great hesitancy to actually allow for change that will bring real discipleship—and real disciples. *Strong and Courageous* bridges the gap between talk and action both in terms of audience and content.

The audience is *men* wanting to engage in the man-sized challenges of being increasingly devoted believers of Jesus Christ. In terms of content, the journey through Joshua (*passim*) demonstrates the compelling message that following God is not just a religious mandate—it is messy. Men are attracted to this message. The challenge is to get them to start reading and experience transformation personally as well as in ministry.

—Dr. Bob Wenz
Professor of Christian Thought, The King's University,
and author of *Navigating Your Perfect Storm*

Les Tripp casts new light on the life of Joshua and in so doing, challenges men to step up to their responsibilities as disciples. *Strong and Courageous* applies the trials that Joshua faced to one's spiritual journey and advancing Christ's kingdom.

—Chuck Brewster
Founder and president, Champions of Honor
and author of *Dead Men Rising*

Strong and Courageous is a practical weapon in the arsenal of every man and every ministry to men. Each section is designed to prepare and equip men ready to do battle. Les Tripp understands that when a man wins the battle for his soul, he wins the battles for his marriage, family, faith, and future.

—Dr. Dan Erickson
Chief servant leader, People Matter Ministries,
and author of *Finding Your Greatest Yes*

Les Tripp has given us a timely resource for a timeless need of every man, regardless of his age or level of responsibility and leadership. The title says it all, *Strong and Courageous.* During these troubling times in our churches and our culture, this book will help every man who reads it, "be that guy."

—Marty Granger
Chairman, Foundation for Manhood

Strong and Courageous

A Devotional for Men in the Battle

Les Tripp

WestBow Press books may be ordered through booksellers or by contacting:

WestBow Press
A Division of Thomas Nelson & Zondervan
1663 Liberty Drive
Bloomington, IN 47403
www.westbowpress.com
1 (866) 928-1240

ISBN: 978-1-4908-5262-1 (sc)
ISBN: 978-1-4908-5261-4 (e)

Library of Congress Control Number: 2014916876

Printed in the United States of America.

WestBow Press rev. date: 11/05/2014

Contents

This book is dedicated to the memory of John Gorman who, with the Lord's help, was strong and courageous in the battles of life. He was a faithful servant, a valued prayer and accountability partner whose life caused people to ask about his faith.

I am indebted to two coworkers in the battle for men's souls: Robert Young, my pastor, and Dan Wetzel, vice president of church ministries for the Christian and Missionary Alliance. I appreciate their valuable input on crafting these thoughts.

In addition, Dr. Laura Barnes, Trish Rollins, and Steve Bracken provided excellent suggestions on improving readability. I am also deeply indebted to my daughter, Diane, for editing the manuscript, and Linda, the wife of my youth, whose patience and support were significant in seeing this project through to the end.

Introduction

> "Now fear the Lord and serve him with all faithfulness ... then choose for yourselves this day whom you will serve, ... **But as for me and my household, we will serve the Lord.**"
>
> —Joshua 24:14–15 (emphasis added)

Joshua exhorts Israel and us to choose to serve the Lord. The point is service. Effective service requires making Jesus Christ the Lord of our lives. It takes more than a commitment. It takes surrender. It takes submission. It is about taking discipleship seriously. Engaging in the battle for the souls of men is a choice. This collection of devotional thoughts provides insight into the life of one of the great leaders of the Bible.

I have always been intrigued by the book of Joshua and recently began to focus on the message of the book to contemporary men. I began to see significant principles for developing spiritual maturity and for leading men on their spiritual journeys.

The Joshua narrative is a call to be engaged in the battle. The Lord calls us to lead men to the throne of grace and on to a deeper life in Christ. The Scriptures used are taken from the New International Version unless otherwise indicated.

Over the years, I have collected testimonies from men about what God was doing in their lives. They were collected anonymously to encourage men to share openly about their struggles and victories. I have frequently drawn from these testimonies to illustrate principles under discussion.

When we study Scripture, God asks us to consider the changes He wants us to make in our personal lives as well as our ministry. I will use the phrases looking in and looking out to refer to these challenges. For example:

Looking In: To what degree have you submitted to the Lord? What is more important, doing work for the Lord or drawing closer to the Lord?

Looking Out: Are you leading men to a deeper relationship with Christ?

Concluding each devotional is a New Testament Scripture related to the topic and a brief statement that applies the main thought of the devotion to discipleship. For example:

> All authority in heaven and on earth has been given to me. Therefore go and make disciples of all nations, baptizing them in the name of the Father and of the Son and of the Holy Spirit, and teaching them to obey everything I have commanded you. And surely I am with you always, to the very end of the age.
>
> —Matthew 28:18–20

A disciple chooses to be engaged in the battle for the souls of men.

Focus
Making Jesus Lord

The Rescue

> But the Israelites went through the sea on dry ground, with a wall of water on their right and on their left. **That day the LORD saved Israel from the hands of the Egyptians,** and Israel saw the Egyptians lying dead on the shore.
>
> —Exodus 14:29–30 (emphasis added)

The Lord led the children of Israel from captivity in Egypt (death) and across the Red Sea. He rescued them from Pharaoh's pursuing army. He delivered or saved them from death.

It was God's intention that the Israelites then proceed from the Red Sea into the Promised Land. That is, into a land filled with milk and honey (i.e., into the abundant life). If the Red Sea represents **salvation**, then entering the Promised Land represents **sanctification** or the process of developing a holy lifestyle and effective ministry. Conquering the Promised Land was a discipling process. It involved developing obedience, persistence, boldness, and, most importantly, dependence on God. For us, sanctification involves experiencing the power of God in overcoming obstacles to spiritual growth, being equipped for ministry, and living an empowered life.

Many men are "dead men walking." That is, men destined for eternal damnation. We must build relationships with them and lead them to Christ and the abundant life. We enjoy a life of hope and peace and are called to bring men into a personal relationship with Christ.

Four men met every Sunday morning at 7:00 a.m. to pray for the men in the church. Within six months, one man accepted Christ, another received healing, and a third recommitted his life to the Lord. Prayer is crucial in ministering to men.

Looking In: Have you crossed the Red Sea in your spiritual journey? Have you prepared a testimony about that crossing? Do you cover the before and after differences?

Looking Out: Do you know men who have not crossed the Red Sea? Are you building relationships with them? Are you praying for them?

> In reply Jesus declared, "I tell you the truth, no one can see the kingdom of God unless he is born again." "How can a man be born when he is old?" Nicodemus asked. "Surely he cannot enter a second time into his mother's womb to be born!" Jesus answered, "I tell you the truth, no one can enter the kingdom of God unless he is born of water and the Spirit. Flesh gives birth to flesh, but the Spirit gives birth to spirit."
>
> —John 3:3–6

A disciple is assured of his salvation.

The Preparation

> **The Lord spoke to Moses** in the Tent of Meeting in the Desert of Sinai on the first day of the second month of the second year after the Israelites came out of Egypt.
>
> —Numbers 1:1 (emphasis added)

The Lord guided Israel out of Egypt with the cloud by day and fire by night. He delivered them from Egypt (death). Then the Lord began to affirm their identity as a people set apart. He gave them the Law and established the Levites as priests. He had them construct the Tabernacle and He established His presence in their midst. He provided them with food, water, and direction. They were dependent on Him for provisions and guidance (Ex. 16 through Num. 13).

As with Israel, new believers need to know they are set apart. They need to understand that the Christian life is one of dependence on the Lord, and the Lord wants to be the center of their lives. New believers need to be discipled. They need to be led to know the value of the Word, how to use the Word, who God is, the problem of sin, Jesus' role as Savior, the meaning of salvation, the new life in Christ, the role of the church, and their mission as disciples. A good example to follow is that of a pastor who has made discipling men the cornerstone of his ministry. He disciples men independently over a twelve to sixteen week period. He covers the basics of the faith and then encourages them to engage a third man. The pastor then coaches the first man in the discipling process. Moreover, upon completing the fundamentals, he leads them through character building Scriptures, and in the process helps them develop Bible study skills. His next step is to get them involved in a men's small group. Finally, he invites the willing to participate in a school of ministry where they are equipped to serve in the church and apply their spiritual gifts.

Looking In: Do you understand what it means to be a believer? Do you know how to study and use the Word?

Looking Out: Are you engaged in pursuing the Great Commission? Are you engaged in making disciples? Are you then helping those disciples understand what it means to be a Christian?

> Then he opened their minds so they could understand the Scriptures. He told them, "This is what is written: The Messiah will suffer and rise from the dead on the third day, and repentance for the forgiveness of sins will be preached in his name to all nations, beginning at Jerusalem. You are witnesses of these things. I am going to send you what my Father has promised; but stay in the city until you have been clothed with power from on high."
>
> —Luke 24:45–49

A disciple is well grounded in his faith.

The Rebellion

> That night all the members of the community raised their voices and wept aloud. All the Israelites grumbled against Moses and Aaron, and the whole assembly said to them, "If only we had died in Egypt! Or in this wilderness! Why is the Lord bringing us to this land only to let us fall by the sword? Our wives and children will be taken as plunder. Wouldn't it be better for us to go back to Egypt?" And they said to each other, **"We should choose a leader and go back to Egypt."**
>
> —Numbers 14:1–4 (emphasis added)

In the journey to the Promised Land, the Israelites took a detour—a detour between salvation and sanctification. The Lord, by a powerful display of his authority over nature and man, delivered Israel from Pharaoh and Egypt. In spite of that display of power and their dependence upon God over the following two years, they saw the way ahead leading to death and captivity. The children of Israel did not believe that God would or could overcome the obstacles reported by the ten spies. They saw the challenge through human eyes. The risk was too great; the challenges were monumental. "We cannot do it!" This was a failure of faith. Consequently, they wandered in the desert for the next forty years; it was forty years of anguish and frustration. The people were without rest. The Promised Land was just that: a promise, not a reality. Once the faithless generation passed away, God was ready to try again. Only when disbelief was dead could Israel enter and subdue the Promised Land.

Ministry to men involves leading them to the throne of grace and encouraging or exhorting them to establish a dynamic connection with the Lord. It means being a part of a process that moves them to salvation and onto sanctification. Unfortunately, men frequently spend time in the wilderness. There is a period of wandering yet never arriving. It is a period of spiritual fear, isolation, and loneliness. These men need someone to come alongside them and point the way out of the wilderness into the abundant life.

Looking In: Are you restless in your spiritual journey? Are you still searching? Have you made the transition from salvation to the abundant life, or are you still wandering in the desert?

Looking Out: Do you know believers who do not experience the abundant life—men who are restless in their spiritual journey? Is your ministry designed to take men from the desert to the Promised Land? Have you established relationships in which you can lead men from the desert into the Promised Land?

> "… That is why I was angry with that generation, and I said, 'Their hearts are always going astray, and they have not known my ways.' So I declared on oath in my anger, they shall never enter my rest." See to it, brothers and sisters, that none of you has a sinful, unbelieving heart that turns away from the living God. But encourage one another daily, as long as it is called "Today," so that none of you may be hardened by sin's deceitfulness.
>
> —Hebrews 3:10–13

A disciple believes that God will do it.

Prepare

Qualities for Leading Men
Joshua 1

Four Conversations: The Chain of Command

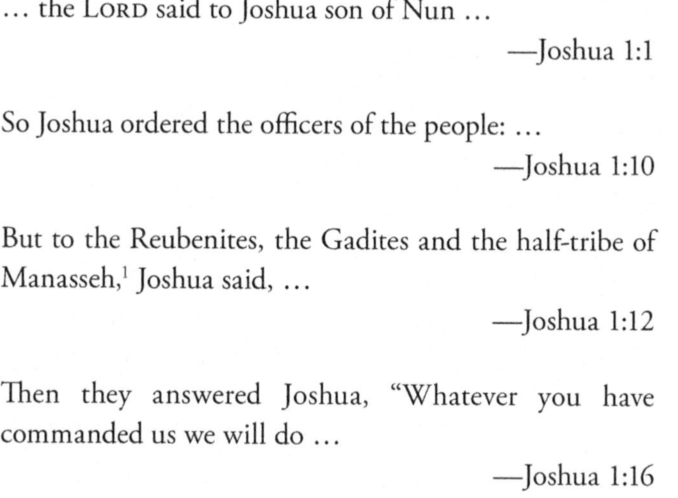

… the LORD said to Joshua son of Nun …

—Joshua 1:1

So Joshua ordered the officers of the people: …

—Joshua 1:10

But to the Reubenites, the Gadites and the half-tribe of Manasseh,[1] Joshua said, …

—Joshua 1:12

Then they answered Joshua, "Whatever you have commanded us we will do …

—Joshua 1:16

The first chapter of Joshua contains four conversations providing twenty qualities required to lead men. These same qualities are threaded throughout Scripture. We see them in the lives of the patriarchs, prophets, kings, apostles, and other leaders. We also see the consequences when they are ignored. They are a key element to advancing the Lord's kingdom through men.

We need to build these qualities into our thoughts and actions. However, if we attempt this without the Holy Spirit, the result will be shallow, fragile, and mechanical. When the Holy Spirit forms these qualities in us, they are deep, durable, and, flow naturally.

When going into battle, there is a natural, scriptural order. When there is a breakdown in that order, disaster follows. The Lord gave His leader initial instructions. Next, His leader instructs men of influence to be ready for action. The leader then instructs those who will lead Israel into the Promised Land—disciplers. Then the disciplers give encouragement to their leader.

Every man stands somewhere in this order. Some are called to communicate God's vision to those who will lead the advance. Others are called to be on the front line of the battle. Still others are called to support the advance. We have a God-given role to play, a calling. We are directed to lead in our homes and be spiritual leaders to those less mature in the faith. At the same time, we are subordinates to the Lord and the spiritual leader(s) He has placed over us.

Looking In: Is the Lord your commander-in-chief? Who is mentoring you?

Looking Out: How are you mentoring a man or men the Lord has given you?

> Paul, an apostle of Christ Jesus by the command of God our Savior and of Christ Jesus our hope, to Timothy my true son in the faith: …
>
> —1 Timothy 1:1–2

A disciple understands the chain of command.

The Lord Directs His Leader

Be Connected

> After the death of Moses the servant of the Lord, **the Lord said to Joshua** …
>
> —Joshua 1:1 (emphasis added)

This is the first conversation in Joshua 1. The Lord instructs Joshua, His leader, in guiding Israel into the Promised Land.

After the death of Moses, the Lord spoke to Joshua. Clearly, Joshua was listening. The old citizen's band (CB) radio jargon was, "Do you have your ears on?" The above verse tells us that Joshua had his "ears on." He was connected to the Lord. He was open to what the Lord was saying. Joshua had the kind of a relationship with the Lord that enabled him to hear God when He spoke. It was not a matter of having to go find God; He was there: *Jehovah Shammah*—Jehovah is there. At other times in the book of Joshua, Joshua sought the Lord (Josh. 5:13–16); however, in this case, the Lord spoke and Joshua heard.

Remember when Samuel was a child and God spoke to him? Samuel did not have the connection that Joshua had, and Samuel needed clarification as to who was calling him.

God speaks to us every second of every day. Becoming a disciple means, like Samuel, learning to hear God's voice. This is a continuing process because we live in a very noisy world. Discerning what is from the Lord and what is not is a challenge. Joshua knew the voice of the Lord. Jesus said that His sheep listen to His voice (John 10:27).

Looking In: Is your relationship with the Lord such that you know He is present? Do you hear Him when He speaks to you? Do you seek Him for guidance, encouragement, affirmation, and accountability on a daily basis? Is your channel to the Lord always open? If not, what is interfering? What can you do to restore or improve communications?

Looking Out: Do you know men who are not connected to God or men who are wandering in the wilderness? Are you connecting and building relationships with them? Are you praying for them consistently? Are you encouraging them in their walk?

> Pray without ceasing.
>
> —1 Thessalonians 5:17

A disciple has calluses on the knees!

Be Ready

> Moses my servant is dead. Now then, you and all these people, **get ready** to cross the Jordan River into the land I am about to give to them—to the Israelites.
>
> —Joshua 1:2 (emphasis added)

This was a change of command. Moses was gone; the Lord placed the mantle of leadership upon Joshua. He commanded Joshua to get the people ready to cross the Jordan and enter the Promised Land. Israel was under new leadership and the new leader was given a mission.

Consider Abram, Moses, David, Isaiah, and the other Old Testament prophets. Consider the disciples in the New Testament. Each was given a mission. We are each given a calling by God. We need to hear that call and respond to it.

At the same time, we encounter changes in leadership in our lives. With new leadership comes new vision, energy, and methods. Joshua was charged with continuing the task the Lord gave Moses. Within the church, the leadership may change but the task remains the same: advance Christ's kingdom.

Looking In: Are you ready for the task the Lord has given you? Are you ready to step out as Joshua did? Perhaps the Lord has placed you under new leadership. Are you ready to move out under that leadership? Are you hesitating or drawing back at new direction? Are you being called out of your comfort zone?

Looking Out: Has the Lord given you a ministry to an individual or to a group? Have you accepted that responsibility? Are you aware that success will only come from the Lord?

> Remind the people to be subject to rulers and authorities, to be obedient, to be ready to do whatever is good, to slander no one, to be peaceable and considerate, and always to be gentle toward everyone.
>
> —Titus 3:1–2

A disciple is ready.

Be a Man of Vision

> I will give you every place where you set your foot, as I promised Moses. **Your territory will extend from the desert to Lebanon, and from the great river, the Euphrates—all the Hittite country—to the Mediterranean Sea in the west.** No one will be able to stand against you all the days of your life. As I was with Moses, so I will be with you; I will never leave you nor forsake you.
>
> —Joshua 1:3–5 (emphasis added)

The Lord's First Promise: The Lord laid out a grand vision for Israel. From a geographical perspective, it must have been beyond their comprehension. They were to seize a vast territory from those who occupied it.

We have received the peace of salvation and enjoy contentment and the knowledge of God's call on our lives. We need to grasp the vision of reaching every man in our sphere of influence. We need to understand that the task ahead is beyond our abilities; it is God-sized. Ministering to men is tough. The battle involves snatching men from the grasp of Satan. We need to be overwhelmed; we need to have a clear picture of where the Lord is leading us and the scope of the task ahead.

Looking In: What challenging vision has the Lord given you? What are the battles you face? What/who are the enemies you face? Do you understand the scope of the battle?

Looking Out: What battles are the men around you facing? Do they know the enemies they face? Are you giving them a vision of what it means to enter the Promised Land?

> He who did not spare his own Son, but gave him up for us all—how will he not also, along with him, graciously give us all things?
>
> —Romans 8:32

A disciple is a man of vision.

Be a Man of Faith

> No one will be able to stand against you all the days of your life. As I was with Moses, so I will be with you; **I will never leave you nor forsake you.**
>
> —Joshua 1:5 (emphasis added)

The Lord's Second Promise: After communicating the vision for the Israelites, God promised that He would be there for them. Do we fully understand that the Lord will be with us, or do we feel we have to fight the battle alone? The Lord says, "Have I not commanded you? Be strong and courageous. Do not be terrified; do not be discouraged, for the LORD your God will be with you wherever you go" (Josh. 1:9). If that is not enough, Jesus told his disciples, "... I am with you always, to the very end of the age" (Matt. 28:20b). Bottom line: you shall overcome (Rom. 8:37)! It is said that the task ahead of us is never greater than the power behind us. Why does God have to keep reminding us that He will not leave or go away from us? "I will never leave you nor forsake you (reject or turn away)" (Deut. 31:6, 8), and "Am I not the God who is close by?" (Jer. 23:23).

Looking In: What obstacle do you face in your personal spiritual journey? Do you believe that the Lord is with you? Do you have faith that He will overcome?

Looking Out: What obstacle do you face in ministering to men? Do you believe that the Lord is with you? Do you have faith that He will overcome?

> Yet he (Abraham) did not waver through unbelief regarding the promise of God, but was strengthened in his faith and gave glory to God, being fully persuaded that God had power to do what he had promised.
>
> —Romans 4:20–21

A disciple knows that God will.

Be Strong and Courageous

> **"Be strong and courageous,** because you will lead these people to inherit the land I swore to their forefathers to give them. "**Be strong and very courageous....**
>
> —Joshua 1:6–7 (emphasis added)

The Lord's first command is to be strong and courageous. Some speculate that Joshua needed this encouragement because he was now the leader of Israel. He was filling Moses' shoes. On the other hand, the Lord knew the challenges that Joshua and the Israelites would face. It takes strength and courage to go into battle as the underdog when the odds are overwhelmingly in favor of the Enemy. No matter how mature we may be in our walk with the Lord, the next task He gives us will be

God-sized. That is why the Lord is always at our side. He will take us through the battle. In sports psychology, the focus is on one's mental state, with emphasis on self-confidence. In matters of the spirit, the focus is on confidence in the Lord. We are to be strong and courageous in the Lord. We will be victorious because we are in Him and He is in us.

Looking In: What are you afraid of? What internal spiritual battles do you face? What new ministry task has the Lord given you? Are these challenges beyond your capability? Are you approaching these challenges in Christ and in the power of the Holy Spirit?

Looking Out: Are you aware of men who need to be reminded that the Lord is on their side? Do you need to come alongside them and encourage them to be strong and courageous?

> Now it is God who makes both us and you stand firm in Christ. He anointed us, set his seal of ownership on us, and put his Spirit in our hearts as a deposit, guaranteeing what is to come.
>
> —2 Corinthians 1:21–22

A disciple is not easily discouraged.

Be Obedient

> … Be careful to obey all the law my servant Moses gave you; do not turn from it to the right or to the left, that you may be successful wherever you go.
>
> —Joshua 1:7

The Lord's second command is to be obedient. Obedience is the key to success. God's instructions focus on the heart (spiritual preparation) and not on swords and shields; so it is with leading men. God focuses on their spiritual preparation as well. Obedience is more important than strategies and tactics. Disobedience undermines our ministry to those who follow us.

Consider the impact of Achan's disobedience: thirty-six men were killed, and the army was routed (Josh. 7:1–5).

The Lord defines success in terms of obedience when he reminds Joshua, "... the LORD your God will be with you wherever you go" (Josh. 1:9). The history of Israel is one of moving between obedience and disobedience, and as a result, victory and defeat. Disobedience invites conflict, creates barriers, and limits the application of God's power. The command is, "Go!" and the promise is, "I will be with you." Dietrich Bonhoeffer said "only the believer is obedient—only the obedient believe."

Those who stand on the outside and look upon the church claim that the church is full of hypocrites. The accusation is true. Paul claimed that the things he did not want to do he did, and the things he needed to do he did not do (Rom. 7:15–20). It is an obedience issue, and obedience comes from submission to the Lord. By submitting, we allow God to do a new work in us. Obedience is a life-long task, but one in which we can have continuing victory in the Spirit.

Today, successful companies place great emphasis on customer satisfaction. We are asked to rate products and services, customer support, and the buying/shopping experience. We serve the risen Lord. How does He rate our service to Him?

Looking In: On a scale of one to ten, what is your obedience rating? In what areas do you need to be more obedient? Is it in the use of your time, your treasure, or your talents? What about disobedience in attitudes, behavior, or thought patterns? Are you bringing these areas under the control of the Holy Spirit?

Looking Out: Are you sharing your struggles with disobedience with another man or men?

> Don't you know that when you offer yourselves to someone to obey him as slaves, you are slaves to the one whom you obey—whether you are slaves to sin, which leads to death, or to obedience, which leads to righteousness? But thanks be to God that, though you used to be slaves to sin, you wholeheartedly obeyed the form of teaching to which you

were entrusted. You have been set free from sin and have become slaves to righteousness.

—Romans 6:16–18

A disciple is obedient.

Be a Man of the Book

> Be careful to obey all the law my servant Moses gave you; do not turn from it to the right or to the left, that you may be successful wherever you go. **Do not let this Book of the Law depart from your mouth; meditate on it day and night, so that you may be careful to do everything written in it. Then you will be prosperous and successful.**
>
> —Joshua 1:7–8 (emphasis added)

The Lord's third command is for Joshua to make the Word an integral part of his life. In reality, God provides Joshua with the key to obedience. The fact that the Lord restates His command in terms of the book of the law emphasizes just how important it is to Joshua's prosperity and success.

Moreover, the Lord exhorted Joshua to be a man of the Word. He made it clear that Joshua's success was dependent on obedience to the Law. "Your word is a lamp to my feet and a light for my path" (Ps. 119:105). The Lord's instructions are intended to encourage, enlighten, and guide. God's leaders are men of the Word. At the end, Joshua prepares the leaders of Israel for his departure and repeats these words. (Josh. 23:6) These words are bookends in the Joshua narrative.

Looking In: Are you a man of the Word? How much time have you carved out of your day to connect with the Lord through His Word? What did He say to you from His Word today?

Looking Out: Have you shared what God is saying with another man? Are the men that you lead men of the Book? Do they give testimony as to what the Lord is saying to them from His Word? Do you ask them what the Lord is saying to them? Are you setting the expectation that the Lord speaks to them personally from His Word?

> All Scripture is God-breathed and is useful for teaching, rebuking, correcting, and training in righteousness, so that the man of God may be thoroughly equipped for every good work.
>
> —2 Timothy 3:16–17

> Jesus answered, "It is written …"
>
> —Matthew 4:4

A disciple is a man of the Word.

Be Strong and Courageous (Again)

> Have I not commanded you? Be strong and courageous. Do not be terrified; do not be discouraged, for the LORD your God will be with you wherever you go."
>
> —Joshua 1: 9

This is the third time in four verses that the Lord exhorted Joshua to be strong and courageous. It is the second time He promises Joshua that He will be with him. Joshua is to be courageous, because the Lord is with him.

Verses 5–9 are in chiastic construction often found in Hebrew and other early writing.

I will never leave you.
    Be strong and courageous.
        Be careful to obey—success will follow.
        Follow the book of the law—prosperity and success will follow.
    Be strong and courageous.
I will never leave you.

This technique serves to reinforce the message and point to the central idea: the command for Joshua to be obedient in all he does. God is adamant, saying, "The task ahead is beyond your capability. Carry it out with boldness because I, the Lord, am not only behind you but I am also beside you and ahead of you. I want this done and will do it. Now be engaged."

Looking In: Are you able to stand with the psalmist when he said, "The Lord is my strength and my shield; my heart trusts in him, and I am helped. My heart leaps for joy and I will give thanks to him in song" (Ps. 28:7). Do you know, at the experience level, that the Lord would not have asked you if it was not something He wanted done and will empower you to do?

Looking Out: Do you have the faith to lead your men with boldness? Are you modeling confidence in pressing on to your God-given goal?

> My purpose in writing is simply this: that you who believe in God's Son will know beyond the shadow of a doubt that you have eternal life, the reality and not the illusion. And how bold and free we then become in his presence, freely asking according to his will, sure that he's listening. And if we're confident that he's listening, we know that what we've asked for is as good as ours.
>
> —1 John 5:13–15 (MSG)

A disciple is bold in serving the Lord.

The Leader to Men of Influence

Be Proactive

> **So Joshua ordered the officers of the people,** "Go through the camp and tell the people, 'Get your supplies ready. Three days from now you will cross the Jordan here to go in and take possession of the land the LORD your God is giving you for your own.'"
>
> —Joshua 1:10 (emphasis added)

This is the second conversation in Joshua 1. It is Joshua, the leader, instructing the officers, men of influence, to get Israel ready for entry into the Promised Land. These were not the men who would lead Israel. Instead, they were given responsibility for organizing the people and getting them ready to advance.

Joshua, having received direction from the Lord, moved forward with confidence. He did not have a clue about how Israel would cross into the Promised Land or how they would subdue the occupants.

So it is with us. When the Lord gives us a task, He expects us to get ready and move out smartly. He expects us to be proactive in pursuing that task. We should not hesitate because of uncertainty over the details in execution. Often the Lord does not reveal the "how" until we act on the "what." The priests had to step into the water before the Lord stopped the flow of the Jordan River (Josh. 3:13).

Linda and I were comfortable where we were. The Lord made it clear that He wanted us in a location halfway across the country. Once we had moved and had settled in, He revealed what it was He wanted us to do. For me it was leading the ministry to men. That was the "what." After three years, we begun to discover the "how" and form a strategy for discipling men in our congregation.

Looking In: What is the ministry the Lord has given you? Are you proactive in overcoming the challenges in your life? Do you believe that the Lord will give you victory in that ministry—even though you are uncertain about how to proceed? Do you understand, at the action level, that He will be with you? What are you waiting for?

Looking Out: Are you aware of issues in the lives of the men around you that hold them back? Are you encouraging them in decision-making and action?

> Therefore, go …
>
> —Matthew 28:19

> For we know, brothers loved by God, that he has chosen you, because our gospel came to you not simply with words, but also with power, with the Holy Spirit and with deep conviction.
>
> —1 Thessalonians 1:4–5

A disciple does not look for a blessing; rather, he looks for opportunities to bless.

Be Ready

> So Joshua ordered the officers of the people, "Go through the camp and tell the people, **'Get your supplies ready.** Three days from now you will cross the Jordan here to go in and take possession of the land the LORD your God is giving you for your own.'"
>
> —Joshua 1:10–11 (emphasis added)

Joshua selected those who were to lead. One of the great themes of Scripture is "be ready" (e.g., Ex. 12:11; Jer. 1:17; Matt. 25:10; and Titus

3:1). In this case, there is a deadline—three days. In other cases, there is uncertainty over when the anticipated event will occur. For example, the wise virgins waiting on the bridegroom (Matt. 25:10) who did not know when he would arrive. Because of uncertainty, the issue is about getting ready. Being ready is a process. Our world, culture, and environment are constantly changing. Being ready yesterday does not mean that we are necessarily ready today. The manna was only good for one day. The message is that the Lord leads us one day at a time.

Getting supplies ready for spiritual battle involves knowing the Word, understanding the Word, and being able to apply the Word. To be ready for spiritual battle, one must spend time in prayer. It means *actively* listening to God. Getting ready for spiritual battle must be intentional, just as it was for Israel.

There is a Himalayan expression: When the expedition is ready, the guide will appear. Francis of Assisi said, "Start by doing what's necessary; then do what's possible; and suddenly you are doing the impossible."

Looking In: Are you ready for the task the Lord has given you? Have you made preparations for what the Lord is going to do? Are your lamps filled (Matt. 25:10)?

Looking Out: How are you helping others prepare for what lies ahead?

> So you also must be ready, because the Son of Man will come at an hour when you do not expect him.
>
> —Matthew 24:44

A disciple is prepared for the task ahead.

Direction to Disciplers

Be Accountable

> But to the Reubenites, the Gadites and the half-tribe of Manasseh, Joshua said, "**Remember the command** that Moses the servant of the LORD gave you: 'The LORD your God is giving you rest and has granted you this land.'"
>
> —Joshua 1:12–13 (emphasis added)

This is the third conversation in Joshua. Joshua instructs those who will actually lead the children of Israel into the Promised Land. The men of Reuben, Gad and the half-tribe of Manasseh are the disciples. They have already settled in their portion of the Promised Land. They have been given rest. They are to lead the other tribes. They are to be disciplers.

Joshua reminded these men of the commitment they had made to Moses when he gave them the lands east of the Jordan River. The Lord expects those faithful to him to follow through on their commitment, i.e., be obedient. Obedience means submission. With God-given rest comes responsibility. Jesus reminded Peter that he was to feed His sheep (John 21:15–17). Joshua held the eastern tribes accountable.

Disciplemaking is the process of moving men from turmoil to peace and from peace to contentment (rest). The peace of salvation comes first, and then comes contentment from making Jesus Christ Lord. Those who are being given rest must assist those who have yet to receive rest. Men tend to live compartmented lives. Spiritual maturity involves dealing with those compartments. Pastor Ted Roberts said, "The closer to Christ we are, the more aware we are of our sin." The Lord is saying, "When you make me Lord of your life, I will give you rest," and with rest comes accountability.

That accountability involves modeling personal growth and leading others to rest. We are accountable to the Lord—and to the men we serve.

There are three important levels in male relationships. The first is acceptance: approval or favorable regard. The second is affirmation: an upholding acknowledgement or positive response to a person's actions. The third is accountability: a mutual agreement to hold each other to an agreed upon standard of behavior. I know a man who struggles with gender identity. I can accept him. I cannot affirm his behavior and there can be no accountability.

Looking In: What is God calling you to do? Are you in an accountability relationship? As a matter of spiritual discipline, do you review accountability questions regularly? Is your walk with God such that He alerts you to sin?

Looking Out: Are you encouraging your men to be in an accountability relationship?

> Brothers, each man, as responsible to God, should remain in the situation God called him to.
>
> —1 Corinthians 7:24

A disciple is accountable.

Be at Rest

> But to the Reubenites, the Gadites and the half-tribe of Manasseh, Joshua said, "Remember the command that Moses the servant of the LORD gave you after he said, 'The LORD your God **will give you rest** by giving you this land.' Your wives, your children and your livestock may stay in the land that Moses gave you east of the Jordan, but all your fighting men, ready for battle, must cross over ahead of your fellow Israelites. You are to help them **until the LORD gives them rest**, as he has done for you, and until they too have taken possession of the land the LORD your God is giving them.

—Joshua 1:12–15 (emphasis added)

Twice during this dialogue Joshua uses the word rest. He describes the state of the eastern tribes as being given rest because they had their allotted land. Then he describes the future state of those who were yet to enter the Promised Land. Joshua tells them to stay with their brothers until they were being given rest.

Rest is a common theme in the Bible. It is defined as a state of inner peace or security. The Hebrew word for rest is *noah*. It means the guaranteed continuance of hope and the assurance of being with the Lord in eternity. *Noah* is an instrument of deliverance; a place or position in which to settle down, a home. It means rest and salvation.[2] Rest is knowing the presence of the Lord. It is, however, the Lord who gives rest. It is not something we achieve on our own (Josh. 1:15). Note that the giving of rest is a continuing process, not a one-time event. "The fear of the Lord leads to life. Then one rests content, untouched by trouble" (Prov. 19:23).

The eastern tribes were being given rest. Therefore, the dialogue between Joshua and these men provides insight into the qualities of those who lead their brothers into rest or the Promised Land.

Looking In: Is the Lord giving you rest? Are you in the Promised Land and dealing with the "occupants." With the Lord's help, are you driving them out?

Looking Out: Do you know men who are not being given rest? What are their names? Are you leading them into their Promised Land?

> "Come to me, all you who are weary and burdened, and I will give you rest. Take my yoke upon you and learn from me, for I am gentle and humble in heart, and you will find rest for your souls. For my yoke is easy and my burden is light."
>
> —Matthew 11:29–30

A disciple has secured rest in the Lord.

Be a Guide

> Your wives, your children and your livestock may stay in the land that Moses gave you east of the Jordan, but all your fighting men, ready for battle, must **cross over ahead of your brothers.**
>
> You are to help them.
>
> —Joshua 1:14 (emphasis added)

Joshua instructed the men of the Reubenites, Gadites, and the half-tribe of Manasseh to lead Israel across the Jordan and into the Promised Land.

After crossing the Jordan, the army would be engaging the enemy. Since these tribes knew what it meant to be receiving rest, Joshua placed them on point, the most vulnerable position. They were to take the risk of being in front.

As leaders of men, we are called to be on point. We need to lead the platoon, the company, or the battalion. We are to show the way. As a result, we are visible and risk taking fire. By being in front, leaders of men protect those who follow, and those who may not be mature enough to understand attacks. Leaders also know how to respond to these followers.

Moreover, those in front frequently draw fire from opponents. We need to be intentional in our efforts to bring men before the throne of grace and encourage them to be stalwart soldiers. We must mentor our men and model behavior that invites others to join the adventure.

You are entering unknown territory (See Josh. 3:4). Guiding is not just a matter of knowing where you are going, but of knowing that God is leading the way and will be giving rest to those who follow.

Looking In: Who is leading you? Who is mentoring and encouraging you?

Looking Out: Who are you leading into rest? Who in your sphere of influence has yet to enter the Promised Land? Leading a men's ministry is about individuals, not an organization.

> Opponents must be gently instructed, in the hope that God will grant them repentance leading them to a knowledge of the truth, and that they will come to their senses and escape from the trap of the devil, who has taken them captive to do his will.
>
> —2 Timothy 2:25–26

A disciple leads.

Be a Team Player

> "… but all your fighting men, ready for battle, must cross over **ahead of your brothers. You are to help them …**"
>
> —Joshua 1:14 emphasis added

Joshua directed the eastern tribes to join and work with the other tribes of Israel, encouraging them in subduing the Promised Land. Joshua directed the fighting men to help the Israelites conquer the Promised Land. It was a matter of everyone working together: those with the inheritance and those yet to receive it. They were to share the burden. God expects those to whom He is giving rest to wage war alongside those yet to receive rest. The conquest must be undertaken by all Israel. The command was to "help your brothers."

It took a team to fight Joshua's battles; it will take a team to fight ours. We are not all wired the same way. We are called to different roles, and the Holy Spirit gifts us for those roles. In the course of ministering to men, we are called to connect, encourage, and exhort. It is not necessary that all the functions of the team be performed by one man. We are to live the call together. We must grow in the Lord together.

For some reason, some men think they can fight the battles of life alone. Men do not ask for directions, right? The role of those who are being given rest is to help their brothers who have yet to receive rest. The battles of life are never intended to be fought in isolation. We need each other. Ministering to men requires teamwork: teamwork in leadership, teamwork in outreach and evangelism, and teamwork in encouraging spiritual growth.

Looking In: What is your role? What is your calling? Are you a coach, a quarterback, a defensive end, a wide receiver, or some other player? What is your grace gift? (Rom. 12:6–8). What are your body gifts? (1 Cor. 12:28–31).

Looking Out: Who is on your team? What are their spiritual gifts? What are the misunderstandings that arise from the application of grace gifts? Are you aware of the Enemy's attacks on your men? Are you teaming against those attacks in prayer, encouragement, and perhaps even exhortation?

> From him the whole body, joined and held together by every supporting ligament, grows and builds itself up in love, as each part does its work.
>
> —Ephesians 4:16

A disciple is a part of the team.

Be Persistent

> "... **until the Lord gives them rest, as he has done for you, and until they too have taken possession of the land** that the Lord your God is giving them. After that, you may go back and occupy your own land, which Moses the servant of the Lord gave you east of the Jordan toward the sunrise."
>
> —Joshua 1:15 (emphasis added)

Joshua told the Reubenites, Gadites, and the half-tribe of Manasseh that they needed to stay until the job was done.

The job is tough. It is challenging. There will always be a temptation to give up and to move on to something easier. Joshua urged the eastern tribes to keep at it until the land had been subdued.

Never give up. Keep on keeping on. The task of encouraging men to move from where they are to where the Lord wants them is difficult, particularly when men resist moving out of their comfort zones. Ministry to men is like herding cats. It is draining, exhausting, and discouraging.

The battle for the souls of men is spiritual warfare. The Enemy throws up barriers, distractions, diversions, and setbacks to keep men from realizing their potential and God's plan for them.

The Lord indicates that there may be times when we need to "shake the dust from our shoes" and move on (Matt. 10:14). When do we do that? When we get frustrated? When we just cannot stand it anymore? What if we are approaching the tipping point?

Only the Lord can tell us when it is time to move on. The battle is the Lord's. "Let us not become weary in doing good, for at the proper time we will reap a harvest if we do not give up" (Gal. 6:9). If we grow weary, the battle is our own and we are using *our* energy and applying *our* wisdom and will. That's how we'll know that we have not relied on the Lord. The Lord directs us to keep at it until the land has been subdued. Retirement is not an option. The good news is that the Lord will sustain us.

Looking In: Are you discouraged and frustrated in your ministry? Are you at your wits' end? Do you want to give up? Are you thinking about retiring? Are you growing weary in doing good? Are you ministering from your own wisdom and strength? Are you empowered by the Holy Spirit?

Looking Out: Do you come alongside men who are struggling to succeed in a task? Are you an encourager to men who find the going tough?

> To those who by persistence in doing good seek glory, honor, and immortality, he will give eternal life.
>
> —Romans 2:7

A disciple persists in the task God has given him.

The Disciplers' Response

Be Willing

> Then they answered Joshua, "Whatever you have commanded us we will do, and wherever you send us we will go ..."
>
> —Joshua 1:16

The eastern tribes gave Joshua a positive and encouraging response. They said, "We will!" This is the fourth conversation in Joshua chapter 1.

They were willing to be a part of the conquest of the land promised to the other tribes. They were willing to set aside their own plans and goals for the good of all Israel, for the good of those who had yet to be given rest. They were willing to set aside safety and security for battle. In spite of the challenges that lay ahead, they were willing to step out of their comfort zone. They said, "Yes!" to the battle.

Ministry to men is a tug of war between doing what is easy and doing what is needed. We often set priorities on the basis of risk rather than value. We avoid those things we feel incapable of handling or for which we deem ill-equipped. Ministry to men involves building connections with men, frequently outside of our comfort zone. It involves encouraging men to become disciples. Beware, the excuses are many: "I don't have time," "My schedule is full." Nevertheless, men must still be encouraged to serve, minister, and support the body. They need to be led to hear God's call.

Looking In: Do you understand the task to which God is calling you? Are you holding back because you do not understand how your skills, gifts, and talents fit into that calling? Have you submitted to His will? Are you willing to engage in the battle? The Lord wants to do great things and has provided you the Holy Spirit to achieve them.

Looking Out: Are you encouraging your men to listen to God's call on their lives? Are you urging them to move out of their comfort zone into the battle?

> Now finish the work, so that your eager willingness to do it may be matched by your completion of it, according to your means. For if the willingness is there, the gift is acceptable according to what one has, not according to what he does not have.
>
> —2 Corinthians 8:11–12

A disciple is willing to engage in the battle.

Be Obedient

> "... Just as we fully obeyed Moses, so **we will obey you ...**"
>
> —Joshua 1:17 (emphasis added)

Not only were the eastern tribes willing to follow orders, they made a commitment to follow Joshua. Moses was gone; therefore, they would follow Joshua. Obedience is a major theme in Scripture. The word "obey" appears nearly 150 times in the Bible. Obedience is the key to freedom and success. Disobedience brings captivity and defeat.

The eastern tribes must have thought it through. They will go to the battlefield once again. They had spent forty years in the wilderness following Moses. They fought against Ammon and Bashan and subdued the land east of the Jordan (See Num. 32.) Now the time had come to conquer the land west of the Jordan under Joshua's leadership.

When Jesus is the Lord of our lives, He asks us to set aside things that are important to us in favor of things that are important to Him. It is one thing to be willing, but something else entirely to be obedient. Obedience is putting your body and soul where your mouth and mind are. Willingness is a mental state. Obedience is a state of action.

Looking In: Have you made a personal commitment to follow your spiritual leader? Are you responding to his leadership? Is there a disconnect between willingness and obedience in your life?

Looking Out: Are you modeling obedience in your sphere of influence? Do your men understand what it means to be obedient? Are you encouraging one another to be obedient?

> Because of the service by which you have proved yourselves, others will praise God for the obedience that accompanies your confession of the gospel of Christ, and for your generosity in sharing with them and with everyone else.
>
> —2 Corinthians 9:13

A disciple is obedient.

Be an Encourager

> "… Only may the LORD your God be with you as he was with Moses … Only be strong and courageous!"
>
> —Joshua 1:17

The men of the eastern tribes encouraged Joshua with a commitment to obey. They capped their response by reminding Joshua that he was operating under God's agenda, authority, direction, and presence.

Those to whom God is giving rest, He expects to be encouragers of those who have yet to receive rest. There are two forms of encouragement: words and action. Action involves working with and walking alongside a brother.

In ministering to men, we face obstacles, barriers, and challenges. We face the forces of darkness. Satan will actively interfere with spiritual growth. Men need to be encouraged in their walk. As leaders of men, we need to say, "Be strong and courageous." We need to convey the message in both words and actions. Be transparent. Let men know that you have faced or are facing challenges. Men are encouraged when they know that we have been there or are facing challenges in our own lives.

At one of our annual men's national leadership meetings, eighteen men participated, seven who had not attended before. The men had carved out a weekend from their busy lives and had traveled from various parts of the United States to take part. It was good to see their passion for ministering to men. I was particularly encouraged by their positive contributions as we set a course for the next five years. Encouragement often comes in the form of the presence of others and their active, positive sharing in developing ministry strategy.

Looking In: Are you using the fact that you do not have the gift of encouragement as an excuse? Have you chosen to be an encourager?

Looking Out: Are you an encourager? Who around you needs a word of encouragement? What about your pastor or other leaders in the church? They can always use a word of encouragement.

> But encourage one another daily, as long as it is called Today, so that none of you may be hardened by sin's deceitfulness … And let us consider how we may spur one another on toward love and good deeds, not giving up meeting together, as some are in the habit of doing, but encouraging one another—and all the more as you see the Day approaching.
>
> —Hebrews 3:13; 10:24–25

A disciple is an encourager.

Be On Guard

> Whoever rebels against your word and does not obey it, whatever you may command them will be put to death.
>
> —Joshua 1:18

There will always be those who revolt when the going gets tough. The Reubenites, Gadites, and the half-tribe of Manasseh were experienced enough to know that rebellion was serious and had to be eliminated or it would undermine the effectiveness of the army. Rebels must be eliminated.

Scripture warns us to be on guard. The position of watchmen is featured prominently in the Scripture. Watchmen were posted on the hills overlooking the battlefield. They were posted on the walls of the city to alert the people when an attack was eminent. Watchmen were posted in vineyards when the fruit was ripe and ready to be harvested. They guarded against those who came at night to steal the fruit.

Have you seen churches disintegrate or split because men rise up against their pastor or the leadership team or fail to stand firm when leaders are under attack? The Devil is the divider. God unites.

As leaders, we need to have discernment. We need to not only know when a man or men are rebelling against the leadership or the direction of the church, but we also need to take action to remove those who are poisoning the atmosphere or are barriers to progress.

Looking In: Do you spend time in the Word? Do you measure your own attitudes and behavior against Scripture? Are you allowing the Holy Spirit to keep you in check?

Looking Out: Do you have the courage to act, to follow through when you are aware of divisive attitudes and behavior? Are you willing to stand up and commit to your leaders that you will not accept those who undermine and oppose the way the Lord is leading the body? Are you a watchman?

> Even from your own number men will arise and distort the truth in order to draw away disciples after them. So be on your guard!
>
> —Acts 20:30–31

A disciple guards the truth.

Be Strong and Courageous (Once Again)

> Only be strong and courageous.
>
> —Joshua 1:18

This is the fourth time in eighteen verses that the words "be strong and courageous" are spoken. The first three are exhortations from the Lord to Joshua. In spite of the challenges that lay ahead, the Lord states that He is the One giving the Land to Israel (vs. 2) and that He is always with them (vs. 9). This time, the phrase "be strong and courageous" is encouragement to Joshua by the men of the eastern tribes.

Then the men of the eastern tribes told Joshua that they would obey him, follow him willingly, and guard against those who would undermine his authority. They concluded their response with a benediction, "only be strong and courageous."

There are three types of strength: physical, mental, and spiritual. Peter speaks of strength in terms of perseverance or steadfastness (See 2 Pet. 1:6). Our natural response to difficult situations is "I can't do it!" or "That's impossible!" True, we cannot. We need to rely on the Lord.

God wants us to do the impossible. It is tough to change our attitudes and behavior. It is tough to encourage men to move from where they are to where the Lord wants them. It is a matter of transferring control to the Holy Spirit. The courage we need comes from the Lord. It is not something we generate ourselves.

Joshua was going to lead Israel on a difficult journey. These men did not know exactly where they were going or how they would get there. They understood the broad objective, not the details. Yet, they made a commitment to follow Joshua. In essence, they were saying, "We are with you. Therefore, be strong and courageous!"

As a leader, it is always good to know that there are those behind us who are partners in ministry and offer encouragement.

Looking In: What is the goal of the task that the Lord has given you? Are you willing to follow, even though you do not know the details? Are you moving forward on your own strength, or are you depending on the Lord to make the way? Are you aware of the Lord working through you? Are you strong and courageous?

Looking Out: Do you stop to encourage your leaders? Do your leaders know that you are there for them? Are you demonstrating willingness in actions as well as words? Do you understand how tough they have it? Do you stand by them? Do you follow their lead willingly? Or do you hold back? If so, why? Do your words and actions say, "Be strong and courageous"?

> Be on your guard; stand firm in the faith; be courageous; be strong.
>
> —1 Corinthians 16:13

A disciple is strong and courageous.

Believe

Step Out in Faith
Joshua 2:1 – 5:12

Experience God's Power

> ... You are to help [your brothers] until the LORD gives them rest, as he has done for you, and until they too have taken possession of the land the LORD your God is giving them ...
>
> —Joshua 1:14b–15a

The first chapter of Joshua focuses on the qualities of those who are being given rest. These are qualities important in spiritual leadership. The Lord and Joshua and the leaders address the state of mind and heart required for helping others to achieve the abundant life and attaining victory in the battles of life. There is no discussion of strategies and tactics. It is a look forward to the rest that will be given to the remaining nine and one half-tribes who had yet to enter the Promised Land. The next four chapters address what it takes to enter into the Promised Land—the abundant, spirit-filled life. They had to:

- Catch the vision
- Follow God's instructions
- Mark the miracle
- Submit to the Lord

These chapters are about a spiritual transition, a transition from where Israel was to where God wanted Israel to be. They are about God's powerful response to Israel's faith. They are about Israel's trust and obedience that unleashed God's power over nature.

God always wants to move us from where we are to where He needs us to be.

Looking In: Are you making the transition to where God needs you to be? Have you caught the vision? Are you moving out in obedience and faith? Do you have a testimony about the power of God in your life? What changes has He made?

Looking Out: Do you see the men around you who have not made the transition to where God wants them? Are you encouraging or exhorting your men to take a step of faith into the abundant life? Are you helping them open their lives to the power of God?

> I have given you authority to trample on snakes and scorpions and to overcome all the power of the enemy; nothing will harm you. However, do not rejoice that the spirits submit to you, but rejoice that your names are written in heaven."
>
> —Luke 10:19–20

A disciple knows that the power behind him is always greater than the challenge ahead.

Catch the Vision

Assess the Path Ahead

> So they went, and came to the house of a harlot named Rahab, and lodged there.
>
> —Joshua 2:1

The Israelites were camped at Shittim on the plains of Moab, east of the Jordan. Just as Moses sent spies into the Promised Land, Joshua needed to know what to expect when they would cross into the Promised Land.

In discipling men, we need to gain insight into their belief systems and strongholds. Strongholds and incorrect belief systems must be confronted by both the disciple and the discipler in order for them to advance as soldiers of Christ. This reconnaissance takes place in the course of building relationships with those we are discipling.

A man reported that he needed to come under the authority of the Holy Spirit and be renewed. In the course of that renewal, the Lord impressed upon him that there were habits and behaviors that were not glorifying Him. He was challenged to live a spirit-filled life and be fruit bearing (See Galatians 5:22–24).

Looking In: Do you routinely stop to evaluate your own life? What are the obstacles, barriers, thoughts, and behavior patterns that are holding you back?

Looking Out: Have you taken the time to get to know the men you are discipling? Do you know the challenges and struggles they are facing? Are you open about your own struggles?

> For this is why I wrote, that I might test you and know whether you are obedient in everything.
>
> —2 Corinthians 2:9 (ESV)

A disciple seeks to understand those whom he is being called to disciple.

Stand Out

> The king of Jericho was told, **"Look, some of the Israelites have come here tonight to spy out the land."** So the king of Jericho sent this message to Rahab, "Bring out the men who came to you and entered your house, because they have come to spy out the whole land."
>
> —Joshua 2:2–3 (emphasis added)

The spies entered Jericho in secret, yet the authorities knew who they were and why they were there. The men apparently stood out from the people. The word of their arrival traveled quickly, even as to where they were. Jericho understood the threat posed by the presence of spies from the invading army.

When stepping into the world, we need to evaluate the men around us. We need to determine their spiritual condition and their openness to the gospel. In that process, we are called to stand out. As believers, we are different, and that difference needs to show.

While waiting in line to be served, a man found a one hundred dollar bill on the floor. He asked if anyone had dropped any money. Getting a negative response, he gave the money to the clerk, who told him that the money was his if no one claimed it within thirty days. Upon returning to work, a coworker reported that he had received a call from a friend who had observed what had happened and commented on the man's integrity. Clearly, that honest man stood out from the crowd.

We witness to others by our actions. We are not always aware of those to whom we witness. (No one claimed the money, so it was his.)

Looking In: As a disciple of the Lord, do you stand out from the crowd?

Looking Out: Do your men stand out from the crowd or do they try to blend in?

> They recognized that they had been with Jesus.
>
> —Acts 4:13 (ESV)

> **A disciple is not created to fit in, but to stand out.**
>
> —Dan Erickson

Believe

> But the woman had taken the two men and hidden them. She said, "Yes, the men came to me, but I did not know where they had come from. **At dusk, when it was time to close the city gate, they left. I don't know which way they went. Go after them quickly. You may catch up with them"** (But she had taken them up to the roof and hidden them under the stalks of flax she had laid out on the roof.) So the men set out in pursuit of the spies on the road that leads to the fords of the Jordan, and as soon as the pursuers had gone out, the gate was shut.
>
> —Joshua 2:4–7 (emphasis added)

Scripture stands so clearly against lying that we miss the fact that, in her lie, Rahab was repudiating her religion and her culture. She placed herself in grave danger by lying. Had the spies been discovered, Rahab would have been considered a traitor. She was harboring the enemy. Her lie illustrates her commitment to the Lord. She aligned herself with the God of Israel. It seems she had made a commitment to the Lord before the arrival of the spies (Joshua 2:8–12).

She believed that the God of Israel was more powerful than the gods of Jericho. Yet there may have been doubt, a carryover from the inadequacy of the gods of Jericho. Clearly, she doubted that the God of Israel could protect the spies. Therefore, she needed to help God by lying. She had faith, but only to a point.

Despite her limited faith, Rahab is in the lineage of the Messiah (Matt. 1:5), is in the faith hall of fame (Heb. 11:31), and was considered righteous (James 2:25).

Looking In: As a disciple of the Lord, what would you have done if you were in Rahab's position?

Looking Out: Where are your men in their faith? Do they try to help God out when they get in a tight situation? Are you encouraging them in their faith?

> He replied, "Because you have so little faith. I tell you the truth, if you have faith as small as a mustard seed, you can say to this mountain, 'Move from here to there' and it will move. Nothing will be impossible for you."
>
> —Matthew 17:20

A disciple not only believes; he knows that God will.

Live in Hope

> … a great fear of you has fallen on us, so that all who live in this country are melting in fear because of you. We have heard how the Lord dried up the water of the Red Sea for you when you came out of Egypt, and what you did to Sihon and Og, the two kings of the Amorites east of the Jordan, whom you completely destroyed … Now then, please swear to me by the Lord that you will show kindness to my family, because I have shown kindness to you. **Give me a sure sign that you will spare the lives of my father and mother, my brothers and sisters, and all who belong to them, and that you will save us from death."**
>
> —Joshua 2:9–13 (emphasis added)

Word traveled far and fast. Rahab had accurate knowledge of the Lord's triumphs. The Israelites were victorious over Sihon and Og and she and the Canaanites knew they were next. As Rahab indicates, the Canaanites were more afraid of the God of Israel than the rag-tag army of Israel. They were aware that the Lord was behind Israel's victories. Jericho was a great fortification, yet the king and the people were in great fear.

There is a clear contradiction here. The Canaanites, Rahab included, understood that their gods were no match for the God of Israel. Yet the Canaanites were going to hold fast to their belief system in spite of pending death and destruction. The truth was hidden from the Canaanites: the God of Israel was Lord over all. Rahab knew the truth! She made a great confession of faith. Only Rahab went over to the Lord's side and took her family with her.

Looking In: As a disciple of the Lord, are you abandoning the belief systems of our culture? Have you fully gone over to the Lord's side? Have you placed your full trust in the Lord?

Looking Out: Are the men in your sphere of influence living in hope or defeat? Do they live in fear in these times, or do they look forward to the promise of enjoying Christ forever? Are you encouraging them in their journey of faith?

> May the God of hope fill you with all joy and peace as you trust in him, so that you may overflow with hope by the power of the Holy Spirit.
>
> —Romans 15:13

A disciple lives in hope, not fear.

Be Assured

> Now then, please swear to me by the Lord that you will show kindness to my family, because I have shown kindness to you. **Give me a sure sign** that you will spare the lives of my father and mother, my brothers and sisters,

> and all who belong to them, and that you will save us from death." "Our lives for your lives!" the men assured her. "If you don't tell what we are doing, we will treat you kindly and faithfully when the LORD gives us the land." The men said to her, "This oath you made us swear will not be binding on us unless, when we enter the land, you have tied this scarlet cord in the window through which you let us down, and unless you have brought your father and mother, your brothers and all your family into your house. As for anyone who is in the house with you, his blood will be on our head if a hand is laid on him. But if you tell what we are doing, we will be released from the oath you made us swear." "Agreed," she replied. And she tied the scarlet cord in the window.
>
> —Joshua 2:12–21 (emphasis added)

More than a third of the narrative relating to the spies is devoted to the contract between Rahab and the spies. Rahab had transferred her faith from the gods of Jericho to the God of Israel. Not being an Israelite, she needed confirmation or assurance that she and her family were under the protection of the God of Israel.

The spies directed Rahab to testify to her conviction in three ways. She had to hang a scarlet cord out of her window. Then she needed to bring her family under the eternal protection of the Lord, starting with calling them to her house and keeping them there. Finally, she was not to reveal why the spies had come.

Looking In: Have you received the assurance of your salvation? Do you know for certain that you are saved? Have doubts about your eternal future been eliminated?

Looking Out: Are you encouraging your family to seek salvation from the Lord? Are you leading others to the foot of the cross and then to the assurance of their salvation?

> And this is what God has testified: He has given us eternal life, and this life is in his Son. So whoever has God's Son has life; whoever does not have his Son does not have life. I write this to you who believe in the Son of God, so that you may know you have eternal life.
>
> —1 John 5:11–13 (NLT)

A disciple directs new believers to assurance in their new faith.

Make Your Faith Obvious

> The men said to her, "This oath you made us swear will not be binding on us unless, when we enter the land**, you have tied this scarlet cord in the window through which you let us down,** … So she sent them away and they departed. **And she tied the scarlet cord in the window.**
>
> —Joshua 2:17–21 (emphasis added)

Protective Covering. There is a parallel between the scarlet cord, the blood placed over the doorways in Egypt (Ex. 12:22–23), and the blood shed by Jesus on the cross. All were a protective covering. If Rahab hung a scarlet cord from her window, the army of Israel (certain and approaching death) would pass over her and her family. By hanging the cord, she brought her family under the atoning blood of Christ.

Obedience. Rahab hung the scarlet cord in the window immediately after sending the spies on their way. She did not know when the army was going to attack. In fact, she told the spies to hide for three days. Did she think she might forget? Was she like the wise virgins who were prepared for the bridegroom? Or was that cord a sign to the Lord of her submission?

Risk. Rahab had already been questioned about the spies. Now she was hanging a very obvious sign from a window in the wall of the city. What was she thinking by calling attention to herself? She made her faith obvious.

A lady tried to sell a man something at the mall at Christmas time. She asked him, "Do you celebrate Christmas?" He replied, "I celebrate Jesus!" He said that she choked! When she recovered, she asked him if he was Christmas shopping and looking for something for his wife. He said, "No, I am walking through the mall talking to God!" He said no thanks to the gift suggestions and left wondering what she must have been thinking!

Looking In: Have you placed yourself under the atoning blood of Jesus Christ? Are you hesitant to make a statement for Christ? Are you willing to take a risk for Christ?

Looking Out: Do you know men who hesitate to take a stand for the Lord? Are you encouraging them in their faith?

> First, I thank my God through Jesus Christ for all of you, because your faith is being reported all over the world.
>
> —Romans 1:8

A disciple is not afraid to make his faith obvious.

Have Faith

> I know that the LORD has given this land to you … When the LORD gives us the land … The LORD has surely given the whole land into our hands …
>
> —Joshua 2:9, 14, 24

Verse 8 says the Lord carries through on His promises. He promised Israel the Promised Land (Gen. 28:15; 50:24; Ex. 3:17; 13:11; 32:13). Rahab knew of this promise and believed it. She transferred her trust to the God of Israel. The people of Jericho obviously had the same information as Rahab, but refused to transfer their trust to the God of Israel.

In verse 14, the spies' response was, "When the Lord gives us the land …" They had faith the Lord was going to give them the land. They were not waiting until they got home and put the matter to a vote by the governing body. The spies' statement, in the context of the contract with Rahab, was an oath. It was not to be taken lightly.

Verse 24 says that unlike the spies of forty years earlier, these spies reported that the Lord had already given the land to them. Their report indicates that Israel had learned the lesson of forty years in the desert. Did the spies know better than to give a pessimistic report to Joshua, who forty years earlier along with Caleb, reported that the Lord would give them the land?

"Now faith is being sure of what we hope for and certain of what we do not see" (Heb. 11:1). The children of Israel were commended for having faith for the victory before they even fought the battle. The Lord has a prosperity plan for us as well (See Jer. 29:11). The Lord wants us to step out in faith, particularly when the task seems impossible. The Lord wants us not only to believe that He will do it, but to believe He has already done it.

Looking In: Do the actions of your life represent faith that God will do what He has called you to do? Have you hung out your scarlet cord? If not, what are you waiting for?

Looking Out: Are you sharing with your men ways they can hang out the scarlet cord? How do you encourage the men in your sphere of influence to listen and step out in faith on God's call on their lives? Do you remind them that the Lord will give them the victory?

> I tell you the truth, anyone who has faith in me will do what I have been doing. He will do even greater things than these, because I am going to the Father. And I will do whatever you ask in my name, so that the Son may bring glory to the Father. You may ask me for anything in my name, and I will do it.
>
> —John 14:12–14

A disciple acts on the Lord's promises.

Follow God's Instructions

Put the Lord in Front

> Early in the morning Joshua and all the Israelites set out from Shittim and went to the Jordan, where they camped before crossing over. After three days the officers went throughout the camp, giving orders to the people, "When you see the ark of the covenant of the LORD your God, and the priests, who are Levites, carrying it, you are to move out from your positions and follow it. **Then you will know which way to go, since you have never been this way before. But keep a distance of about a thousand yards between you and the ark; do not go near it."**
>
> —Joshua 3:1–4 (emphasis added)

First, the leaders instructed the people to follow the ark of the covenant across the river. The ark represented the presence of the Lord and was carried by Levites. It would show the way. The Lord calls us to go where we have never been before. For some, as in this case, the move is geographical. For others it may be a new ministry in the same place.

Second, The Lord instructed Israel to put the ark in a vulnerable position. Protection for the ark, the army, was one thousand yards away. Consider Uzzah who died because he tried to steady the ark (2 Sam. 6:6–7). God and God alone will protect His presence.

Third, the ark was set apart from the people. It was in clear view of the people as they crossed the river. As long as they could see the presence of the Lord, they knew they were on the right path. The Lord points the way.

Looking In: Do you put the Lord in front of everything you do? Do you ever get ahead of the Lord? Do you launch before praying? When the Lord asks you to do the impossible, He does not leave you to your own devices. Do you try to help God by using your own solutions in life and ministry, or do you trust the Lord to work through the power of the Holy Spirit? Do you keep Him "in sight?" Is he "visible" as you move forward?

Looking Out: What is your testimony about prayer in your daily life? Do you make praying the first part of an accountability relationship? Do the men around you recognize the need to put the Lord first?

> And he withdrew from them about a stone's throw, and knelt down and prayed, saying, "Father, if you are willing, remove this cup from me. Nevertheless, not my will, but yours, be done." And there appeared to him an angel from heaven, strengthening him.
>
> —Luke 22:41–43

A disciple starts everything with prayer.

Be Spiritually Prepared

> Joshua told the people, "Consecrate yourselves, for tomorrow the LORD will do amazing things among you."
>
> —Joshua 3:5

Joshua alerted the Israelites that the Lord was going to do great things in their midst. They needed to be consecrated in preparation for what He was about to do. Consecration was needed to prepare the people to see God in action. Consecration is a matter of focus, or centering down. For Israel, it meant cleansing, washing one's clothes, and abstaining from sexual relations (Ex. 19:14–15). It meant purification.

The reason we may not see God at work is because we are not spiritually prepared. God is always at work. "But Jesus answered them, "My Father has been working until now, and I have been working."" (John 5:17 NKJV)

During an emphasis on the deeper life, a man wrestled with the concept of Spirit control. A few nights later, he lay awake in bed for several hours while the Lord revealed what He had been doing in the man's life. It was a time of uninterrupted and focused closeness with God. For him, it was the beginning of putting the Lord in front.

We need to be consecrated—spiritually prepared—to see God doing great things.

Looking In: What is God doing in your life? Are you aware that He is at work? Are you aware that He wants to do great things? Are you prepared spiritually to see what God is doing? What steps do you take to prepare yourself to see what God is doing?

Looking Out: What response do you get when you ask men what God is doing in their lives? What do they share when you ask what the Lord has said to them from His Word? Are you intentional in encouraging your men to listen, watch, and see God at work?

> … but in your hearts regard Christ the LORD as holy, always being prepared to make a defense to anyone who asks you for a reason for the hope that is in you.
>
> —1 Peter 3:15 NKJV

A disciple centers on the Lord.

Move Out in Proper Order

> Joshua said to the priests, "Take up the ark of the covenant and pass on ahead of the people." So they took it up and went ahead of them.
>
> —Joshua 3:6

> The men of Reuben, Gad and the half-tribe of Manasseh crossed over, armed, in front of the Israelites, as Moses had directed them.
>
> —Joshua 4:12

Joshua instructed the priests carrying the ark of the covenant to lead in crossing the Jordan. The crossing was to start with the presence of the Lord leading the way. The Lord wants to lead the way in our lives.

The armed men of the Reubenites, Gadites, and half-tribe of Manasseh were instructed to follow the ark. Those who had already been given rest were to lead the nine and one half-tribes who had yet to be given rest.

We are called to position ourselves between the Lord and those we disciple. We look to the Lord as we lead others to the throne of grace and onto the abundant life. In disciplemaking, we are called to be a bridge between the Lord and those we disciple.

Looking In: Have you established a proper order in your life? Have you placed the Lord in front of your efforts, activities, and decisions? Have you been intentional in allowing Him to lead you moment-by-moment, day-by-day?

Looking Out: Do your efforts, actions, and decisions testify that God is leading you? Do you share how God is leading you with the men in your sphere of influence? Are you encouraging your men to develop the discipline of putting the Lord first?

> Now to him who is able to keep you from stumbling and to present you blameless before the presence of his glory with great joy, to the only God, our Savior, through Jesus Christ our Lord, be glory, majesty, dominion, and authority, before all time and now and forever. Amen.
>
> —Jude 1:24–25

A disciple follows the Lord and leads others.

Be Exalted

> And the Lord said to Joshua, **"Today I will begin to exalt you in the eyes of all Israel, so they may know that I am with you as I was with Moses …**
>
> —Joshua 3:7 (emphasis added)

> That day the LORD exalted Joshua in the sight of all Israel; and they revered him all the days of his life, just as they had revered Moses.
>
> —Joshua 4:14,

The Israelites were moving on under new leadership. Moses was gone. Joshua was now their leader. The Lord knew that the people needed confirmation that Joshua was to lead them into the Promised Land, just as He had selected Moses to lead them. This was not for Joshua's benefit. It was because God would be glorified through Joshua's leadership. The message was to both Joshua (I will be with you as you lead the people) and the people (Joshua is your leader).

At the Red Sea, the Lord parted the waters when Moses lifted his staff. However, at the Jordan, the Lord stopped the water when the priests stepped into and stood in the river. Once across the Jordan, the people held Joshua in awe, just as they had Moses. The Lord exalted Joshua in the eyes of the people because he demonstrated knowledge of God's plan and directed its execution. God demonstrated awesome power over nature because of Joshua's obedience. The people saw what the Lord had done because they had followed Joshua.

Looking In: Have you experienced God's anointing in leadership? Does that anointing drive you to your knees in complete submission? Are you seeing people respond to your ministry? Is the Lord using you to accomplish His mission? Are you seeing the Holy Spirit at work when you exercise your spiritual gifts?

Looking Out: What evidence do you see in leaders around you that they have been anointed by God? Is God glorified? Is the Lord doing great things through them?

> Whoever exalts himself will be humbled, and whoever humbles himself will be exalted.
>
> —Matthew 23:12

A disciple is exalted by the Lord.

Make Him the Lord of Your Life

> Tell the priests who carry the ark of the covenant: 'When you reach the edge of the Jordan's waters, go and stand in the river.'" Joshua said to the Israelites, "Come here and listen to the words of the LORD your God. This is how you will know that the living God is among you and that he will certainly drive out before you the Canaanites, Hittites, Hivites, Perizzites, Girgashites, Amorites and Jebusites. See, the ark of the covenant of **the LORD of all the earth will go into the Jordan ahead of you**.
>
> —Joshua 3:8–11 (emphasis added)

The Lord of all the earth was a far different concept than that held by the occupants of Canaan. In the cultural context we saw in chapter 2 with Rahab, the Lord was the God of Israel and the Canaanites had their own gods. Israel was coming from and preparing to enter a land with people who worshiped their own gods. The Lord commanded, "You shall have no other gods before (or, besides) me."

We live in a culture with many gods. We need to be constantly reminded and aware that the Lord is God of all. Anything else is a distraction.

A man attended sessions on the deeper life. He came to understand that he should not seek God's help in wrestling with unhealthy behavior and thought patterns. Instead, he should seek Spirit-control in these areas. The man experienced victory in these areas of his life by praying for Spirit-control when facing temptations. He was learning to put the Lord first.

Looking In: What are the things in your life that distract you from the Lord of all the earth? Are those distractions the gods of our culture: money, power, possessions, popularity, and position? Do you make a habit of taking an inventory of the things you pursue that take the place of the Lord of all the earth? What do you place in front of you as you proceed through each day? Is it the Lord or is it what our culture considers important?

Looking Out: Do you make the distractions of our culture a matter of accountability? Do you address cultural distractions when you gather with your men? Are you aware of the things the men around you consider important: money, power, possessions, popularity, and position?

> But I do not account my life of any value nor as precious to myself, if only I may finish my course and the ministry that I received from the LORD Jesus, to testify to the gospel of the grace of God.
>
> —Acts 20:24

A disciple has no other god than the Lord of all the earth.

Step Out in Faith

> "… Tell the priests who carry the ark of the covenant: 'When you reach the edge of the Jordan's waters, go and stand in the river.'" Joshua said to the Israelites, "Come here and listen to the words of the LORD your God. This is how you will know that the living God is among you and that he will certainly drive out before you the Canaanites, Hittites, Hivites, Perizzites, Girgashites, Amorites and Jebusites. See, the ark of the covenant of the LORD of all the earth will go into the Jordan ahead of you. Now then, choose twelve men from the tribes of Israel, one from each tribe. **And as soon as the priests who carry the ark of the LORD —the LORD of all the earth—set foot in the Jordan, its waters flowing downstream will be cut off and stand up in a heap."**
>
> —Joshua 3:8–13 (emphasis added)

Joshua informed the people that God, the Lord over all the earth, would do mighty things in their midst. The Lord would clear the way across the Jordan at flood stage. This was going to be a sign that He intended and was able to drive out the inhabitants of the Promised Land.

But first, the priests would have to step into the river. They had to step out in faith!

A man had been out of work for several months. Due to his background, he had difficulty getting a job. On a Wednesday evening, he prayed about the situation with several brothers in Christ. Unbeknownst to him, a member of the congregation arranged for him to fill a job opening. He began work the following Monday on a job for which he had neither applied nor interviewed.

Looking In: Are you facing an "impossible" task? Are you facing a challenge that discourages you from moving forward? Is it a marriage or family issue? Is it a task or relationship at work? Is it a ministry challenge? What is keeping you from stepping out in faith?

Looking Out: We are commanded to make disciples. We are called to move men from the bleachers onto to the spiritual playing field. Does the task ahead seem impossible? What are the obstacles in getting started? Are you ready to step out in faith, believing that the Lord will give you victory?

> ... that your faith might not rest in the wisdom of men but in the power of God.
>
> —1 Corinthians 2:5

A disciple steps out in faith.

Depend on the Lord

> So when the people broke camp to cross the Jordan, the priests carrying the ark of the covenant went ahead of them. Now the Jordan is at flood stage all during harvest. Yet as soon as the priests who carried the ark reached the Jordan and their feet touched the water's edge, **the water from upstream stopped flowing. It piled up in a heap a great distance away, at a town called Adam in the vicinity of Zarethan, while the water flowing down to the Sea of the Arabah (the Salt Sea) was completely cut off. So the people crossed over opposite Jericho.** The priests who carried the ark of the covenant of the

> Lord stood firm on dry ground in the middle of the Jordan, while all Israel passed by until the whole nation had completed the crossing on dry ground.
>
> —Joshua 3:14–17 (emphasis added)

When the people crossed the Red Sea, there was water on both sides and Pharaoh's army pursuing them. The only way to escape death was to move forward. The Lord created a path for that escape.

When the people crossed the Jordan River, there was no water in sight. Death was not a factor. The people moved across voluntarily. They were not under duress. We need to learn that God does not do things the same way twice.

The Lord pushed the water back twenty miles upstream at flood stage. He did it when the priests stepped into the river. The Lord opened the way into the Promised Land. He was giving the Israelites a dramatic demonstration of His power in preparation for the battles that lay ahead. He gave them access to the abundant life.

According to ancient pagan traditions of judgment, by passing though water safely, the Israelites were declared innocent; therefore, this was a message to the inhabitants of the land. Moreover, Israel was absolved of the rebellion forty years earlier. They crossed on dry ground.

Looking In: Is the God who does the impossible the God you are depending on in your personal battles? Do you believe that He can do the impossible? Do you believe that God wants the best for you? Do you believe that He is committed to advancing His kingdom through you? Are you prepared to see God work in new ways? Are you prepared to see God do great things?

Looking Out: Where are the men around you? Have they crossed the Red Sea? Have they crossed the Jordan? Have you made it a priority to encourage these men in their walk? Are you being intentional in that effort?

> If God is for us, who can be against us?
>
> —Romans 8:31

A disciple depends on God.

Advance Together in Faith

> So when the people broke camp to cross the Jordan, the priests carrying the ark of the covenant went ahead of them. Now, the Jordan is at flood stage all during harvest. Yet as soon as the priests who carried the ark reached the Jordan and their feet touched the water's edge, the water from upstream stopped flowing. It piled up in a heap a great distance away, at a town called Adam in the vicinity of Zarethan, while the water flowing down to the Sea of the Arabah (the Salt Sea) was completely cut off. So the people crossed over opposite Jericho. The priests who carried the ark of the covenant of the LORD stood firm on dry ground in the middle of the Jordan, **while all Israel passed by until the whole nation had completed the crossing on dry ground**.
>
> —Joshua 3:14–17 (emphasis added)

At Kadesh-barnea the people rebelled in unity (except for Joshua and Caleb), and the Lord delayed their entry into the Promised Land. Now, together they crossed the Jordan into the Promised Land.

The Israelites made a visual statement by moving across the Jordan. They were saying, "Together, we are advancing into the land that the Lord is giving us. Together we will advance under the power of God." They knew that the journey ahead would not be easy. Many battles would be needed to clear the land of its occupants. The task would not be easy. Regardless, they moved forward together.

While the Lord calls us to individual tasks within the body of Christ, He calls the body to advance His kingdom. We let petty differences, distractions, and doubts hinder our advance as a body of believers. We are a people empowered by God to advance His kingdom.

Looking In: Do you let petty differences, doubts, and distractions keep you from being a part of the unified body of believers? Are you a part of the problem or a part of the solution?

Looking Out: Is there a lack of unity among the believers around you? What is the issue: lack of faith, personal agendas, or the absence of commitment? Are you gently encouraging those who are holding back? Are you helping the men develop a dynamic relationship with the Lord?

> May the God who gives endurance and encouragement give you a spirit of unity among yourselves as you follow Christ Jesus, so that with one heart and mouth you may glorify the God and Father of our Lord Jesus Christ.
>
> —Romans 15:5–6

A disciple seeks unity among believers.

Mark the Victory

Remember

> When the whole nation had finished crossing the Jordan, the LORD said to Joshua, "Choose twelve men from among the people, one from each tribe, and tell them to take up twelve stones from the middle of the Jordan from right where the priests stood …" So Joshua called together the twelve men … and said to them, "Go over before the ark of the LORD your God into the middle of the Jordan. Each of you is to take up a stone on his shoulder, … They took twelve stones from the middle of the Jordan, … as the LORD had told Joshua; **… And Joshua set up at Gilgal the twelve stones they had taken out of the Jordan.**
>
> —Joshua 4:1–10; 19–20 (emphasis added)

The Lord told Joshua to build a monument to mark the place where the Israelites had crossed the Jordan. The stones came from the middle of the river—a reminder that the Lord had cleared a dry path. The Lord was saying, "This is a milestone in your spiritual journey. I cleared the way for you in power and grace." The stones were a reminder and a message to "all the peoples of the earth." In future challenges and impossibilities, God would make a way.

This is the first of seven memorials established by Israel during the conquest of the Promised Land. The markers reflect the important stages in entering and subduing the land.

God has plans for us. He will accomplish them. And when He does, He expects us to set markers as reminders of His plan and power and as a testimony to others. The first thing we need to mark is the peace (rest) that comes with making Jesus the Lord of our lives. God is great! Celebrate His Lordship.

Looking In: Have you set markers in your life: salvation, making Christ the Lord of your life, physical or emotional healing, restoration of relationships, victory over bondage, success in an endeavor, etc.? Do you keep reminders of these events? Have you noted them in your journal? Do you move against challenges with faith in God?

Looking Out: What are the markers in the life of your community of believers? What has God done in your midst? Are they setting "stones" as reminders of God's plan and His power to accomplish it? Are you encouraging your men to set markers in their own lives?

> This is the disciple who is bearing witness about these things, and who has written these things, and we know that his testimony is true.
>
> —John 21:24

A disciple sets spiritual markers in his life.

Explain It

> "... Each of you is to take up a stone on his shoulder ... to serve as a sign among you. In the future, when your children ask you, 'What do these stones mean?' **tell them** that the flow of the Jordan was cut off before the ark of the covenant of the Lord. When it crossed the Jordan, the waters of the Jordan were cut off. These stones are to be a memorial to the people of Israel forever."
>
> —Joshua 4:5–7 (emphasis added)

> He said to the Israelites, "In the future when your descendants ask their fathers, 'What do these stones mean? tell them ...'"

—Joshua 4:21–22

In verses 6–7, Joshua provides the rationale for establishing a memorial to the crossing. He speaks as a leader to leaders. The leadership needs to understand what must be done and why.

In verses 21–24, Joshua explains the memorial to the people. His explanation begins with the present and moves to the future. It is not only a reminder to the people, but also a reminder to future generations.

At times, the Lord gives us general directions. He points us in a direction and then fills in the details as we go. At other times, He gives us details at the outset. The Great Commission is general: "make disciples as you go!" Then as we go, He points us toward the people with whom He wants to deal (through us). Often, what the Lord asks us to do may not be clear at the outset. But, He will fill in the details as we move out in obedience.

Looking In: Do you hear God speak? What is He saying during prayer? What is He saying from His Word? What is He saying through other people? Are you listening?

Looking Out: As a ministry leader, are you careful to explain what needs to be done and why it is needed? Do you make sure that those working with you understand?

> Then Peter began to explain it to them, step by step, saying, "I was in the city of Joppa praying, and in a trance I saw a vision…." When they heard this, they were silenced. And they praised God, saying, "Then God has given even to the Gentiles the repentance that leads to life."
>
> —Acts 11:4–5, 18

A disciple explains vision, insights, needs, and actions.

Live in the Presence of the Lord

> So they took it up and went ahead of them.

—Joshua 3:6

> Now the priests who carried the ark remained standing **in the middle of the Jordan** until everything the LORD had commanded Joshua was done by the people, just as Moses had directed Joshua. The people hurried over, **and as soon as all of them had crossed, the ark of the LORD and the priests came to the other side** while the people watched.
>
> —Joshua 4:10–11 (emphasis added)

> Then the LORD said to Joshua, "Command the priests carrying the ark of the Testimony to come up out of the Jordan." So Joshua commanded the priests, "Come up out of the Jordan." And the priests came up out of the river carrying the ark of the covenant of the LORD. No sooner had they set their feet on the dry ground than the waters of the Jordan returned to their place and ran at flood stage as before.
>
> —Joshua 4:15–18

These verses recap, with additional details, the Jordan crossing. Step by step the Lord directed the crossing. Once the people had crossed, He instructed the priests carrying the ark of the covenant to move out of the river to the west bank. The ark led the way, was in the middle, and then came behind. God was present at the beginning, in the middle, and at the end of the crossing—*Jehovah Shammah*—the Lord is there (Ezek. 48:35; Ps. 23:4).

Looking In: Do you experience God's presence in all that you do? Does He lead you in your actions? Is He there in the middle? Are you aware of Him at the end? God is always at work. Have you seen Him in the rearview mirror? Do you, like Brother Lawrence, "practice the presence of God"?[3]

Looking Out: Do you experience God at the beginning, middle, and end of your ministry endeavors and life's challenges? Are you sharing this with your men?

> Abide in me, and I in you. As the branch cannot bear fruit by itself, unless it abides in the vine, neither can you, unless you abide in me. I am the vine; you are the branches. Whoever abides in me and I in him, he it is that bears much fruit, for apart from me you can do nothing.
>
> —John 15:4–5

A disciple abides in Christ.

Reboot

> **On the tenth day of the first month** the people went up from the Jordan and camped at Gilgal on the eastern border of Jericho.
>
> —Joshua 4:19 (emphasis added)

The Israelites entered the Promised Land at the beginning of the year. The tenth day of the first month of the year was also the day that the sacrificial lamb was to be selected for the Passover (See Ex. 12:3). Passover was to be celebrated four days later. For the Israelites, this moment launched a new generation, a new year, a new land, a new beginning, and the first Passover in forty years (Josh. 5:10). For Israel, this was a reboot.

The first Passover preceded their escape from Egypt (death) at the Red Sea. The first Passover was an action that looked forward to their salvation. On the tenth day of the first month, Israel began preparations for the Passover at Gilgal. It was to be a Passover looking back; looking back on their entrance into a land flowing with milk and honey. It represented the completion of the first step in receiving the abundant life. God's intention is that people not only be saved, but that they also have the abundant life. The Gilgal Passover was a celebration of their new life.

Reboot is a verb that means to boot (a computer system) again. Gilgal was a reboot for Israel. When the Lord acts in our lives, He wants us to reboot. He deals with us through miracles, His Word, and interaction with other believers. He calls us to start anew when we encounter a truth that is new to us, or when we apply a truth to our lives. When we reboot, we need to celebrate the new work the Lord is doing or has done. We also need to share what He is doing with others. In this sharing, we are exercising an encouragement gift for the common good (1 Cor. 12:7–11).

Looking In: When the Lord does a new thing in your life, do you consciously and intentionally celebrate what He has done? Do you take the time to prepare for that celebration? Do you stop to thank the Lord? Is it more than a quick thank you?

Looking Out: When the Lord does a new work in your community of believers, do you stop to consciously and intentionally celebrate what He has done?

> And we also thank God constantly for this, that when you received the word of God, which you heard from us, you accepted it not as the word of men but as what it really is, the word of God, which is at work in you believers.
>
> —2 Thessalonians 2:13

A disciple takes time to reflect on God's great mercy and grace.

Advance toward the Challenge

> On the tenth day of the first month the people went up from the Jordan and camped at Gilgal on the eastern border of Jericho.
>
> —Joshua 4:19

Gilgal is about three miles northeast of Jericho and several miles from the Jordan River. Jericho was the first challenge the Israelites faced after crossing the Jordan, and Israel moved *toward* that challenge, not away from it. They were on the path set by the Lord. Once before, they were on God's path and they rebelled. This time they were obedient.

God's path is seldom easy. It often takes us to places we do not want to go or into situations we want to avoid. If we find life or ministry easy, we may not be on God's path. God's plan included Jericho. Jericho was an obstacle to the occupation of the Promised Land. It was an obstacle that

Israel had to overcome. So it is with our lives. There are obstacles we need to overcome. God needs us to overcome them.

A man struggled to live a more structured life—that was his challenge. Nothing seemed to work until he set an overarching goal of making a difference in the lives of others. Once that became his focus, other areas of his life began to fall into place.

The Lord's plan (challenge) is for us to make a difference in the lives of other people. Is that not the Great Commission—go and make disciples? What happens in our lives when we make the main thing the main thing? We will encounter barriers. Someone said that if we do not encounter Satan in our lives, maybe we are moving in the wrong direction.

Looking In: Are you on God's path? If so, He will lead you to confront the things in your life that hinder your spiritual growth and your ministry. It has been said the closer we are to Christ, the more aware we are of our sins. Are you becoming more aware of your sin?

Looking Out: What are the obstacles in our ministry? Are you moving to them intentionally or are you avoiding them?

> Rather, as servants of God we commend ourselves in every way: in great endurance; in troubles, hardships and distresses; in beatings, imprisonments and riots; in hard work, sleepless nights and hunger; in purity, understanding, patience and kindness; in the Holy Spirit and in sincere love; in truthful speech and in the power of God; with weapons of righteousness in the right hand and in the left; through glory and dishonor, bad report and good report; genuine, yet regarded as impostors; known, yet regarded as unknown; dying, and yet we live on; beaten, and yet not killed; sorrowful, yet always rejoicing; poor, yet making many rich; having nothing, and yet possessing everything.
>
> —2 Corinthians 6:4–10

A disciple moves toward challenges.

Be Empowered

> "In the future when your descendants ask their fathers, 'What do these stones mean?' tell them, 'Israel crossed the Jordan on dry ground.' For the LORD your God dried up the Jordan before you until you had crossed over. The LORD **your God did to the Jordan just what he had done to the Red Sea when he dried it up before us until we had crossed over**. He did this so that all the peoples of the earth might know that the hand of the LORD is powerful and so that you might always fear the LORD your God."
>
> —Joshua 4:21–24 (emphasis added)

The Lord prepared Israel to enter the Promised Land at Kadesh-barnea and promised to go with them. There was no river to cross, nor was there a pursuing army. God intended it to be a smooth transition from two years of preparation in the desert to the Promised Land and the abundant life. However, Israel believed the task was too hard. They rebelled and spent the next forty years in the desert.

In contrast, entry from Shittim required crossing a river at flood stage. Israel literally had to take a step of faith. Moreover, God had to open the way. This was a new generation, a people who, with the exception of Joshua and Caleb, had not crossed the Red Sea. While God had met their needs in the desert, they had not experienced God's awesome power over nature as had the earlier generation at the Red Sea.

Also, recall that the successful Jordan (water) crossing was a message to the inhabitants of the land that Israel had been declared innocent according to ancient tradition.

Looking In: Where have you seen God's awesome power in your life (e.g., salvation, the abundant life, healing, victories over bondage, success in an endeavor)? Where have you seen Him do the impossible?

Looking Out: Do the men in your sphere of influence understand the need to move from where they are to where God wants them to be? Do they understand that God will make a way? Have they experienced a

Jordan crossing in their lives? Are you encouraging your men toward a deeper relationship with the Lord?

> Without weakening in his faith, he [Abraham] faced the fact that his body was as good as dead—since he was about a hundred years old—and that Sarah's womb was also dead. Yet he did not waver through unbelief regarding the promise of God, but was strengthened in his faith and gave glory to God, being fully persuaded that God had power to do what he had promised.
>
> —Romans 4:19–21

A disciple reflects on God's power in his life.

Submit to the Lord

Spread the Word

> Now when all the Amorite kings west of the Jordan and all the Canaanite kings along the coast **heard how the LORD had dried up the Jordan** before the Israelites until we had crossed over, their hearts melted and they no longer had the courage to face the Israelites.
>
> —Joshua 5:1 (emphasis added)

The word had spread. The God of Israel was awesome. He had done a mighty thing in stopping the river at flood stage. Israel did not spread the word. Israel did not have contact with the occupants of the land. The occupants, however, were watching.

Moreover, the kings were comparing the power of the Lord to the power of their gods and their hearts melted. Had their gods done anything like what the Lord had done? For them there was no hope.

Hopelessness is a contagious disease; therefore, we are called to carry the message of hope to a dying world. Every day we face people who need the message of hope in their marriages, work, and personal relationships. We are called to spread the word about His great works—in our own lives and in the lives of others. God did the impossible. He asks us to do it, not because we can do it, but because He wants to do it. As difficult as it may be, let's just do it and give Him the credit! He wants the credit.

A man was assisting with disaster recovery in a creative access country (a country where access must be gained by means other than missionary visa). He noticed hopelessness among both the people and the leadership.

He began sharing the message of hope. It opened the door to presenting the gospel to local people as well as government leaders.

Looking In: What is the Lord doing in your life? Are you aware of what He is doing? Do you give testimony about what the Lord is doing?

Looking Out: What is the Lord doing in the lives of men around you? Do you take time to share what He is doing? Do you make that a matter of routine?

> To each is given the manifestation of the Spirit for the common good.
>
> —1 Corinthians 12:7

A disciple hears, sees, and shares what God is doing.

Fear the Lord

> Now when all the Amorite kings west of the Jordan and all the Canaanite kings along the coast heard how the Lord had dried up the Jordan before the Israelites until we had crossed over, **their hearts melted and they no longer had the courage to face the Israelites**.
>
> —Joshua 5:1 (emphasis added)

The kings of the region feared the Israelites because of what the God of Israel did. The people of the area already knew about the Red Sea (Josh. 2:8–10). The miracle of the crossing was another example of the power of the God of Israel.

There are two types of fear: a fear that results in withdrawal and a fear that brings us to our knees in reverence and obedience. Chapter 5 is about both types of fear. The kings of the region recoiled in terror. The Israelites responded in reverence and obedience.

"Fear Not" is repeated 365 times in Scripture. The reference is to terror. Terror is immobilizing. It creates a sense of helplessness and loss of courage. It is a barrier to an effective response.

On the other hand, Scripture tells us that "the fear of the Lord is the beginning of knowledge ..." (Prov. 1:7). As disciples, we are to advance in the face of challenges and barriers, empowered by the Holy Spirit, and in the confidence that the Lord is in the battle with us. Fear of the Lord leads to a clear vision. We receive insight both into our calling, and into how we are to advance.

Looking In: Does seeing the mighty hand of God in your life put you on your knees?

Looking Out: Who do you know who needs to see the mighty hand of God? Are you coming alongside them to encourage, support, and be there for them? Are there men around you who need to move from fear to hope?

> David said about him:
> "'I saw the LORD always before me.
> Because he is at my right hand,
> I will not be shaken.
> Therefore my heart is glad and my tongue rejoices;
> my body also will live in hope,
> because you will not abandon me to the grave,
> nor will you let your Holy One see decay.
> You have made known to me the paths of life; you will fill
> me with joy in your presence.'"
>
> —Acts 2:25–28

A disciple fears the Lord.

Trust the Lord

> ... their hearts melted and they no longer had the courage to face the Israelites.
>
> —Joshua 5:1

The reaction of the kings is another example of cultural boundaries. Like the people of Jericho, they could not think about leaving their gods who were clearly no match against the God of Israel. Unlike Rahab (Josh. 2:18–14), they were not willing to transfer their trust to the God of Israel. They were not aware that they had a choice. In many cases, men are not willing to alter convictions, even when faced with overwhelming evidence to the contrary. Winston Churchill said, "Men occasionally stumble over the truth, but most of them pick themselves up and hurry off as if nothing happened."

Many in our society stumble over the truth when they encounter believers. Some hurry on, oblivious to a life of faith. Clearly, they are not open to the gospel. Others begin to question the differences they see in the lives of believers. We need to be sensitive to these people. They may be open to hearing our testimony. We should not be among those who see opportunities and hurry on.

A friend of mine reported that the Lord had given him a ministry in a very dark chat room. He clearly does not fit in with those who visit that chat room. He reported that he has been thrown out many times because he shares the gospel. However, at this writing, ten people have prayed with him to receive Christ. These new believers are from Illinois; Ohio; Michigan; the provinces of New Brunswick and Ontario in Canada; India; Scotland; and England. My friend is moving into dangerous territory, but he is trusting in the Lord.

Looking In: Are you prepared to alter your convictions, or are you subconsciously bound to old patterns of thinking or the way our culture responds to overwhelming challenges? Transferring trust is a day to day and moment-by-moment, conscious decision.

Looking Out: Do you know men who are not aware they have a choice between eternal death and eternal life, or a choice between just existing and living the abundant life?

> May the God of hope fill you with all joy and peace as you trust in him, so that you may overflow with hope by the power of the Holy Spirit.
>
> —Romans 15:13

A disciple is an instrument for leading others to transfer trust to the Lord.

Be Unique

> At that time the LORD said to Joshua, "Make flint knives and circumcise the Israelites again." **So Joshua made flint knives and circumcised the Israelites** at Gibeath Haaraloth (hill of foreskins).
>
> —Joshua 5:2–3 (emphasis added)

> This *is* My covenant which you shall keep, between Me and you and your descendants after you: Every male child among you shall be circumcised; and you shall be circumcised in the flesh of your foreskins, and it shall be a sign of the covenant between Me and you.
>
> —Genesis 17:10-11

Circumcision was the first of two steps in preparing the men of Israel for the battles that lay ahead. It was an act binding the men into the service of the Lord and a prerequisite for the Passover. It was the physical indication of their spiritual submission. It was the mark of their personal commitment to a covenant with the Lord.

Circumcision made the Israelite men unique. It was a part of their identity. Today, we baptize believers as an indication of a personal, conscious commitment to the new covenant. It is an intentional act through which we symbolically participate in the death, burial, and resurrection of Jesus Christ. As it was with circumcision, baptism establishes our identity as believers.

The following story illustrates the importance of identity. Ben was born to Sarah Wade and Dr. L.W. Hooper on October 13, 1870. Hooper refused to marry Sarah because he was engaged to another woman. When Sarah's father died, she placed Ben in an orphanage. Dr. Hooper found and adopted the boy. Throughout his childhood, Ben took heat concerning his parentage. Ben said that these experiences helped him form an identity outside of his parentage and build strong confidence. In fact, these encounters motivated him to excel. He became determined to be best in his class. He graduated from Carson-Newman College in 1890. He was baptized at age fifteen and was staunch in his faith throughout his life. Ben Hooper was governor of Tennessee from 1911–1915.

Looking In: What is your identity? On what is it based? What sets you apart?

Looking Out: Do the men around you understand their uniqueness in Christ? Do they know the significance of being children of God? Are they exercising the spiritual gifts that come with being a part of the family of God?

> But when God, who set me apart from birth and called me by his grace, was pleased to reveal his Son in me so that I might preach him among the Gentiles …
>
> —Galatians 1:15–16

A disciple is set apart.

Be Unencumbered

> At that time the Lord said to Joshua, "Make flint knives and circumcise the Israelites again." So Joshua made flint knives **and circumcised the Israelites** at Gibeath Haaraloth.
>
> —Joshua 5:2–3 (emphasis added)

> **Circumcise your hearts**, therefore, and do not be stiff-necked any longer.
>
> —Deuteronomy 10:16 (emphasis added)

Imagine this: being set apart by removal of the foreskin from a part that was, by God's order, to remain hidden (Genesis 3:20, Exodus 28:42, Leviticus 18:6, and Isaiah 47:3). Moreover, it was the removal of something that had no use or benefit. Today, circumcision is controversial. Yet modern studies indicate a number of significant health issues associated with leaving the foreskin intact. The Lord had more than uniqueness and male health in mind in prescribing circumcision. In Deuteronomy 10:16, the Lord alerts us to the spiritual significance of circumcision. He instructs that the heart be circumcised. That is, the removal of behavior, thoughts, and relationships that are not God honoring or interfere with our relationship with the Lord. Paul makes the distinction between the flesh and the Spirit (Romans 8:1-2). The flesh is a dependence on one's own wisdom and abilities. From Paul's perspective, the circumcision of the heart is the transfer of trust from self to the Holy Spirit. As the Lord reminded Joshua, he was to look neither to the right nor the left (Joshua 1:7). The circumcised heart has blinders.

The circumcision of the heart is a process. As we continue to grow in the Lord, He, through the Holy Spirit, reveals those things that interfere with our relationship with Him.

Note also that the Lord commanded only the males to be circumcised. Men are to lead their families. Therefore they must be set apart before the Lord and not be encumbered with actions, views, and dealings with others that are clearly not God honoring.

Looking In: Are you aware that the Lord is circumcising your heart? What changes is He making? Are you open to the Holy Spirit working in you or through others alerting you to areas of your life that need cleansing?

Looking Out: Do your men know that they need cleaning up? Are they aware of the power of the Holy Spirit to reveal and cleanse their lives? Are they in accountability relationships?

> In Him you were also circumcised with the circumcision made without hands, by putting off the body of the sins of the flesh, by the circumcision of Christ, buried with Him in baptism, in which you also were raised with *Him* through faith in the working of God, who raised Him from the dead. And you, being dead in your trespasses and the uncircumcision of your flesh, He has made alive together with Him, having forgiven you all trespasses, having wiped out the handwriting of requirements that

> was against us, which was contrary to us. And He has taken it out of the way, having nailed it to the cross.
>
> —Galatians 2:11-14 (NKJV)

A disciple welcomes the cleansing power of the resurrection.

Be Protected by the Lord

> At that time the LORD said to Joshua, "Make flint knives and circumcise the Israelites again." So Joshua made flint knives **and circumcised the Israelites** at Gibeath Haaraloth.
>
> —Joshua 5:2–3 (emphasis added)

The act of circumcision at Gibeath Haaraloth made the Israelite army vulnerable to attack. They were, for all practical purposes, defenseless. Circumcision not only set them apart, it was an act of complete trust in the Lord.

While the original occupants of the land may have lacked courage in the face of Israel's God, they could have observed the weakness of the army and seized the opportunity to attack. They did not. They were afraid of the God of Israel, and that fear immobilized them.

On the other hand, the men of Israel certainly were aware that circumcision would make them vulnerable. Yet they proceeded. They trusted the Lord who had just pushed the waters of the Jordan back and made it possible for them to cross on dry ground into the Promised Land.

When we submit to the Lord and are obedient, we are vulnerable. Our words and actions set us apart. Society does not appreciate the fact that we are different. Because we are different, we face criticism, persecution, and even death. We are vulnerable; however, we are called to live under the protection of the Lord.

Looking In: Do you trust the Lord to keep you safe? Are you certain that you will be safe? Do you place yourself in the hands of a loving and caring God? In the face of danger, do you respond with a defensive posture or on your knees?

Looking Out: Do the men in your sphere of influence understand that God is and will be there in their weakness? Are they willing to follow God's direction when it involves being vulnerable?

> But he said to me, "My grace is sufficient for you, for my power is made perfect in weakness." Therefore I will boast all the more gladly of my weaknesses, so that the power of Christ may rest upon me.
>
> —2 Corinthians 12:9

A disciple understands that he is under the protection of the Lord.

Die to Self

> ... until all the men who were of military age when they left Egypt had died, since they had not obeyed the LORD.
>
> —Joshua 5:6

The disobedience of the earlier generation was in the failure to trust the Lord. As the Joshua narrative points out, the disobedient generation was gone. This time, the people were obedient and God did the impossible.

For us, obedience means allowing the Lord to clean us up and empower us for the tasks to which He has called us. It means depending on the Lord for victory: *Jehovah Nissi*, Jehovah my banner. (In Exodus 17:8-16, Moses built an altar in recognition of the victory over Amalek brought by the Lord).

Access to the Promised Land required the death of unbelief. The move from eternal life to the abundant life requires submission to the Lord. Submission to the Lord requires daily denial of self. The Lord requires self-denial so that He can work and be glorified. When self gets in the way, the Lord allows us to do our own thing, and our own thing is not God's thing. To be active tools of the Lord, we need to die to self.

Looking In: Have you chosen the death of unbelief? Are you in the process of getting rid of the baggage you acquired in your life prior to salvation? Have you become obedient, so as to allow God to lead you into the abundant life? Who is in control of your life, you or the Lord?

Looking Out: Do you have a plan for moving a man from salvation to the abundant life? Do you know men who are going through the motions of belief but are not addressing the issues in their lives? Have they died to self?

> I appeal to you therefore, brothers, by the mercies of God, to present your bodies as a living sacrifice, holy and acceptable to God, which is your spiritual worship. Do not be conformed to this world, but be transformed by the renewal of your mind, that by testing you may discern what is the will of God, what is good and acceptable and perfect.
>
> —Romans 12:1–2

A disciple dies to self, daily.

Honor God

> Then the LORD said to Joshua, "Today **I have rolled away the reproach of Egypt** from you." So the place has been called Gilgal to this day.
>
> —Joshua 5:9 (emphasis added)

Reproach is censure, rebuke, and disapproval, making failure more apparent. For Israel, the reproach of Egypt was to escape from Egypt (death) only to die in the desert. Moses confronted the Lord when He was angry with Israel. If the Lord destroyed Israel, He would become the laughing stock of the Egyptians. What benefit was there in Israel being saved from death (given eternal life) but never experiencing the abundant life (the Promised Land)? The Israelites had now entered the Promised Land. The reproach of Egypt was cancelled. Note that the rebellious generation experienced the "reproach of Egypt." They died in the desert.

We are called to glorify God. Our testimony must go beyond salvation. It must express the joy of the abundant life. After facing death in the desert for forty years, the Israelites placed their faith in the Lord, and the Lord gave them the Promised Land (abundant life). It was the Lord who removed the reproach of Egypt. Not the army. Not the people. The Lord moved Israel from defeat to victory.

For us, the reproach of Egypt is the failure to believe that the Lord has much more for us than salvation. And like salvation, He will make the way. We must realize that "he is no fool who gives [up] what he cannot keep, to gain what he cannot lose" as Jim Elliot said. We must move Christ from being a part of our lives to making Him the center of our lives.

Looking In: Has the Lord removed the "reproach of Egypt" from your life? Have you made the transition from believer to submitting servant?

Looking Out: Are you helping the men in your sphere of influence make the transition from salvation to the abundant life? Are you intentional in your efforts? Do you have a plan?

> So let's keep focused on that goal, those of us who want everything God has for us. If any of you have something else in mind, something less than total commitment, God will clear your blurred vision—you'll see it yet! Now that we're on the right track, let's stay on it.
>
> —Philippians 3:15–16, (MSG)

A disciple has moved from accepting Jesus as Savior to making Him Lord.

Remember the Lord's Mercy

> On the evening of the fourteenth day of the month, while camped at Gilgal on the plains of Jericho, **the Israelites celebrated the Passover**.
>
> —Joshua 5:10 (emphasis added)

This was the first Passover since Sinai. The celebration ceased forty years earlier when Israel rebelled over the challenge of entering the Promised

Land. Now the Israelites could celebrate both deliverance from judgment, and access to a land flowing with milk and honey: the abundant life.

The Lord directed that the Passover be repeated annually to be a reminder of what He did in rescuing Israel from Egypt. Under the new covenant, we are commanded to repeat the Lord's Supper as a reminder of what the Lord did for us on the cross; He delivered us from death.

Looking In: Is the Lord's Supper something you do because it is on the calendar? Is it something that has become vain repetition, or is it an act that has personal significance?

Looking Out: What do your men think about the Lord's Supper? Do you discuss it? Do you understand that Christ's broken body and shed blood brings unity to the body of Christ?

> And he took bread, and when he had given thanks, he broke it and gave it to them, saying, "This is my body, which is given for you. Do this in remembrance of me." And likewise the cup after they had eaten, saying, "This cup that is poured out for you is the new covenant in my blood.
>
> —Luke 22:19–20, (ESV)

A disciple grasps the personal significance of Jesus' broken body and shed blood.

Be Empowered

> At that time the LORD said to Joshua, "Make flint knives and circumcise the Israelites again." So Joshua made flint knives and circumcised the Israelites at Gibeath Haaraloth.... On the evening of the fourteenth day of the month, while camped at Gilgal on the plains of Jericho, the Israelites celebrated the Passover.
>
> —Joshua 5:2–3, 10

The Lord directed that the circumcision and the Passover be performed after crossing the Jordan. Logic would indicate that these actions take place on the east side of the river where they were protected. The Lord's message was that the conquest of the Promised Land was to be accomplished by His power, not by the power of men. These two events—circumcision and the crossing of the Jordan—reaffirmed the covenant relationship between the Lord and Israel. Clearly, Israel's commitment to the covenant was essential for possessing the land.

Today we celebrate two ordinances in bringing our lives under a covenant relationship with the Lord: Baptism and the Lord's Supper. Unfortunately, we usually celebrate these activities in the safety of our churches. We may not draw the connection between the covenant and the battles that we face in a pagan culture. At the Lord's direction, circumcision and the Passover preceded Israel's battles. We need to understand that baptism and the Lord's Supper also set the stage for our battles; the battle is the Lord's and not man's.

Looking In: Do you recognize that acknowledging your covenant relationship with the Lord comes before the battle? Are you engaging the Enemy using your own power or the Lord's?

Looking Out: Do the men around you understand the relationship between the covenant and their battles? Are they putting the Lord on point or are they engaging the Enemy on their own?

> ... And a second reminder, dear children: You know the Father from personal experience. You veterans know the One who started it all; and you newcomers—such vitality and strength! God's word is so steady in you. Your fellowship with God enables you to gain a victory over the Evil One.
>
> —1 John 2:13–14, (MSG)

A disciple lives under the covenant and power of the Lord.

Receive the Lord's Provision

> The manna stopped the day after they ate this food from the land; there was no longer any manna for the Israelites, but that year they ate of the produce of Canaan.
>
> —Joshua 5:12

For forty years they had existed on a diet of manna—the same thing for breakfast, lunch, and dinner. It was the same day after day, month after month, year after year. Now they had variety. The Lord provided the manna. Now the Lord provided them with fruit and grain. They did not plant or cultivate it. They ate off the land for a year. The Lord introduced a major change in their daily life. Their faith brought them into a richer life.

If we fail to move from salvation into the abundant life, we are destined to live on the significant, but meager provision of salvation: the same day after day, week after week, month after month, and year after year. We receive only milk, not meat.

Upon deciding to make Jesus the Lord of our lives, we gain access to the abundant life with its variety of fare. We move from milk to meat. The Lord opens His Word to us, and we begin to experience His power in our lives in overcoming sin and advancing His kingdom.

Looking In: Have you made the transition from milk to solid food in your walk with the Lord (1 Cor. 3:2; Heb. 5:12–14)? Are you being fed daily from the Word? Is God opening His Word to you through your quiet time and your study with others? Are you experiencing the riches in His Word?

Looking Out: Do you know men who have not graduated to solid food? Have you built a trusting relationship with one or more of them in order to encourage them to seek a closer walk with the Lord and enjoy the richest of fare (Isa. 55:2)?

> He himself gives life and breath to everything, and he satisfies every need there is.
>
> —Acts 17:25

A disciple feeds on the Word daily.

Overcome

Gain the Victory
Joshua 5:13 – 12:34

Conquer Barriers to Effective Living

> So Joshua subdued the whole region, including the hill country, the Negev, the western foothills and the mountain slopes, together with all their kings. **He left no survivors. He totally destroyed all who breathed, just as the LORD, the God of Israel, had commanded.**
>
> —Joshua 10:40 (emphasis added)

Thus far, we have observed the Lord and Joshua giving guidelines for entering the Promised Land. In chapters 2–5, the narrative describes the miracle of the Jordan River crossing. The message to the Israelites was clear: I am with you and will lead you to victory.

The next seven chapters continue to show God's awesome power in the face of overwhelming obstacles and threats. These chapters also illustrate defeat resulting from disobedience, deception, and self-confidence.

Our personal spiritual journeys are ones of overcoming obstacles, and dealing with issues of willful disobedience and hidden faults. We are living the continuing process of sanctification as the Lord prepares us for ever greater opportunities and challenges. As the Israelites learned on their journey, they would have to transfer trust to the Lord on a daily basis. The spiritual journey must be under the leadership of the Lord. It is the Lord who brings the victory.

Looking In: What are the obstacles in your life that interfere with living the victorious life? Are you actively engaged in eliminating them? Is the Lord leading your efforts, or are you trying to defeat the Enemy on your own?

Looking Out: How are the men in your sphere of influence doing in their battles? Are they seeing victories? Are you a source of guidance and encouragement?

> Through acts of faith, they toppled kingdoms, made justice work, took the promises for themselves. They were protected from lions, fires, and sword thrusts, turned disadvantage to advantage, won battles, routed alien armies. Women received their loved ones back from the dead. There were those who, under torture, refused to give in and go free, preferring something better: resurrection.
>
> —Hebrews 11:33–34, (MSG)

A disciple is aware of the on-going battle.

Understand the Challenge

Ask the Right Question

> Now when Joshua was near Jericho, he looked up and saw a man standing in front of him with a drawn sword in his hand. Joshua went up to him and asked, "Are you for us or for our enemies?"
>
> —Joshua 5:13

Clearly Joshua was focused on capturing Jericho. "How can we subdue the highly fortified city, this stronghold? God, tell me how we can do it."

Joshua demonstrates boldness and faith in approaching a man with a drawn sword. The man's response was blunt, "Neither." The Lord is neither for us nor against us. While Scripture is filled with evidence and promises that the Lord is and will be with us, the question Joshua asks is age old, but it is the wrong question. Are **we** for the Lord or against Him? It is a question of submission. Are we asking God to bless our plans, or are we asking God what His plans are and how we fit into those plans?

We live in a dysfunctional culture; one that has no idea how to deal with challenges or barriers to effective living. Our tendency is to ask, "Why me, Lord?" The battles we face are spiritual. We tend to take them personally. When we do, we succumb to depression, frustration, and despondency. The battle is the Lord's. The solution is submission to the Lord. "Are you for us or against us, Lord?" is not a question of submission. Rather, our response should be, "Lord, advance Your kingdom in this situation. I surrender to You, to Your will." We need to battle the forces of darkness with spiritual weapons.

Looking In: Are you asking the right question? Are you asking the Lord for His plan? Are you open to the Lord working through your challenges?

Looking Out: Are your men asking the right questions? Are your men asking the Lord to join them, or are they asking to join the Lord as He carries out His plan?

> For though we live in the world, we do not wage war as the world does. The weapons we fight with are not the weapons of the world. On the contrary, they have divine power to demolish strongholds. We demolish arguments and every pretension that sets itself up against the knowledge of God, and we take captive every thought to make it obedient to Christ. And we will be ready to punish every act of disobedience, once your obedience is complete.
>
> —2 Corinthians 10:3–6

A disciple seeks the Lord in dealing with strongholds.

Take Your Shoes Off

> The commander of the LORD's army replied, "Take off your sandals, for the place where you are standing is holy." And Joshua did so.
>
> —Joshua 5:15

Joshua formed a posture of reverence—face down. Before the commander of the Lord's army answered, he told Joshua that he was on holy ground. "Take off your sandals …" was not the answer Joshua was looking for.

First, the Lord was meeting Joshua where Joshua was. He did the same with Jacob (Gen. 28) and with Moses at the burning bush (Ex. 3:1–6). The message is that God is not confined to structures made by man.

Secondly, the Lord confirmed Joshua as the leader of Israel in the same way He did Moses a generation earlier. For Joshua, it was not a burning bush; it was a man with a drawn sword.

Third, this verse also teaches us about prayer. To come to God with our problems without first acknowledging him as Lord is foolish. If God dwells in a compartment of our lives, then "taking off our sandals" needs to be an intentional effort. If, on the other hand, the Lord occupies a prominent place in our lives, we will live barefooted before Him. Jesus taught His disciples that when they prayed, they were to acknowledge the Father as the God who is close by (intimate) and far away (in heaven) (Jer. 23:23). We are to hallow (respect) His name. He commands us to meditate upon the one to whom we pray.

Looking In: In the press of life, in facing major obstacles, do you immediately jump into your needs and requests or do you take time to acknowledge the One to whom you are praying? Do you understand that you are on holy ground; that you are entering the presence of the Lord? Does the routine get in the way of the awesome, holy, and almighty Lord? Do you confess that He is God and you are not?

Looking Out: Who in your sphere of influence needs to meet this awesome, holy, almighty Lord? Do you know men who are "at the end of their rope?" Are you encouraging them to acknowledge the Lord and relinquish control? Is this man taking off his sandals?

> … the twenty-four elders fall down before him who is seated on the throne and worship him who lives forever and ever. They cast their crowns before the throne, saying, "Worthy are you, our LORD and God, to receive glory and honor and power, for you created all things, and by your will they existed and were created."
>
> —Revelation 4:10–11

A disciple prays without ceasing.

Eliminate Strongholds

One: Break Down Barriers to Receiving Rest

> **Now Jericho was tightly shut up because of the Israelites. No one went out and no one came in.** Then the Lord said to Joshua, "See, I have delivered Jericho into your hands, along with its king and its fighting men."
>
> —Joshua 6:1–2 (emphasis added)

The history of Israel is the story of spiritual battles, our spiritual battles. Our spiritual battles often involve strongholds, bondages, addictions, persistent and inappropriate behavior, or attitude issues.

Jericho represents a stronghold because there appears to be no possibility of victory. Just as Jericho was "tightly shut up," so it is when we begin to focus on our strongholds. They appear to be impregnable. We encounter great resistance. The result is that we try to break down barriers on our own but it does not work. As a result, we live in a state of defeat.

Clearly, we need to understand that overcoming strongholds requires supernatural power. The battle is spiritual, and therefore, requires spiritual power. It is the Lord's desire that we overcome strongholds. He wants us to be free to advance His kingdom.

A man was drawn into pornography as a boy through exposure to men's magazines and sexual abuse. Although he knew indulging in pornography was wrong and prayed for forgiveness, nothing he did to free himself from the addiction seemed to work. His bondage eventually cost him his marriage and his relationship with his children.

One day a friend suggested he meet with his pastor. This resulted in weekly breakfasts with the pastor at which the pastor just listened and prayed. The man was freed. Now, just as the pastor had done with him, he seeks opportunity to minister to men in the same situation. Prayer is a spiritual weapon.

Looking In: What are the strongholds in your life? Are there things in your life that do not glorify God? Are there things that undermine or destroy your testimony? Make these a matter of persistent prayer as we study the Lord's victory at Jericho.

Looking Out: In most cases, men do not openly share their addictions or bondages. Are you building trust with another man or men so they can be open with you? Are you involved in a Bible study with other men that challenge them to deal with their weaknesses?

> Put on the full armor of God so that you can take your stand against the devil's schemes. For our struggle is not against flesh and blood, but against the rulers, against the authorities, against the powers of this dark world and against the spiritual forces of evil in the heavenly realms.
> —Ephesians 6:11–12

A disciple depends on the Lord to overcome strongholds.

Two: Believe It!

> Now Jericho was tightly shut up because of the Israelites. No one went out and no one came in. Then the LORD said to Joshua, **"See, I have delivered Jericho into your hands, along with its king and its fighting men."**
> —Joshua 6:1–2 (emphasis added)

Jericho stood in the way of full access to the Promised Land. Yet before the people approached Jericho, the Lord said, "I have delivered it into your hands."

God has a plan to prosper us (Jer. 29:11). More importantly, He wants to advance His kingdom through us. He will eliminate the strongholds that stand in our (His) way. He is saying, "I have given you victory over this stronghold."

The Lord has promised to give us victory. "I have given it to you!" Do you believe it?

Looking In: Do you believe that your strongholds have been eliminated in spite of appearances to the contrary? How do you see your strongholds? Are they looming large, or are they defeated and behind you? Has reality overwhelmed your faith? Do you approach challenges in the faith that the Lord has conquered them? Or do you see them from the perspective of your own wisdom and strength?

Looking Out: Who in your sphere of influence is battling a stronghold? Are you praying for him? Are you praying with him? Are you claiming victory together?

> "I tell you the truth, if anyone says to this mountain, 'Go, throw yourself into the sea,' and does not doubt in his heart but believes that what he says will happen, it will be done for him. Therefore I tell you, whatever you ask for in prayer, believe that you have received it, and it will be yours …
>
> —Mark 11:22–14

A disciple is empowered by the Lord to overcome.

Three: Do it God's Way

> "March around the city once with all the armed men. Do this for six days. Have seven priests carry trumpets of rams' horns in front of the ark. On the seventh day, march around the city seven times, with the priests blowing the trumpets. When you hear them sound a long blast on the trumpets, have all the people give a loud shout; then the

> wall of the city will collapse and the people will go up, every man straight in."
>
> —Joshua 6:3–5

Once again, Israel was faced with the impossible. This time it was a highly fortified city. Again, God's instructions did not make sense. At the Red Sea the instructions were, "Strike the water." At Marah, the instructions were, "Throw a log into the water." At Meribah, God said, "Strike the rock." At the Jordan River the instructions were, "Step into the water." At Jericho, God commanded, "March around the city."

Does that make sense? How will marching around the city bring victory? "My ways are not your ways, declares the Lord" (Isa. 55:8–9). God has a different plan. God's action in the past is not an indicator of how He will work now or in the future.

Moreover, by varying man's role, God showed off His power and got the credit. Why then do we hesitate when God asks us to do a task that is beyond us? When the Lord shows us success in one area, do we assume that the same approach will work in another? When the Lord's instructions do not make sense, do we have the faith to proceed?

Looking In: Do you make it a habit to ask the Lord for direction? Do you ask, even when you have done it before? Are you flexible? How do you respond when the Lord's directions do not seem to make sense?

Looking Out: In making disciples, do you think one size fits all? Are you able to be "all things to all men?" (1 Cor. 9:22).

> For the weapons of our warfare are not of the flesh but have divine power to destroy strongholds.
>
> —2 Corinthians 10:4 (ESV)

A disciple seeks and follows the Lord's direction.

Four: Put the Lord on Point

> So Joshua son of Nun called the priests and said to them, **"Take up the ark of the covenant of the Lord and have seven priests carry trumpets in front of it."** And he ordered the people, "Advance! March around the city, with the armed guard going ahead of the ark of the Lord."
>
> —Joshua 6:6–7 (emphasis added)

As at the Jordan, the Lord directed Joshua to place the ark in front of the people. The ark was the presence of the Lord. It was the Lord who was laying siege to Jericho. The fear of the Lord of Israel had the people of Jericho shut up in the city.

When going against strongholds, we must put the Lord in front. It is He who will lay siege to bondage and addictions. Our efforts are weak and ineffective. Storming strongholds requires spiritual weapons. It is the Lord who has the weapons to bring down the barriers.

Looking In: Do you choose to take the Lord into your battles, or try to fight them on your own? What does it mean to put the Lord first? Have you put the Lord on point in your daily life?

Looking Out: Do you emphasize prayer in encouraging your men in their struggles? Do you model prayer before them?

> Those who think they can do it on their own end up obsessed with measuring their own moral muscle but never get around to exercising it in real life. Those who trust God's action in them find that God's Spirit is in them living and breathing God!
>
> —Romans 8:5 (MSG)

A disciple puts the Lord in front of everything.

Five: Persist

> March around the city once with all the armed men. **Do this for six days.** Have seven priests carry trumpets of rams' horns in front of the ark. **On the seventh day, march around the city seven times**, with the priests blowing the trumpets … On the seventh day, they got up at daybreak and **marched around the city seven times** in the same manner …
>
> —Joshua 6:3–4, 15 (emphasis added)

The Israelites marched around Jericho once a day for six days. On the seventh day, they marched around the city seven times. They were persistent. They kept at it. They were determined.

Eliminating strongholds requires persistence. It requires persistence in prayer. We must "march" around the stronghold on our knees. The promise of victory comes through fervent prayer immersed in the belief that God has already brought down the walls.

The Lord's message was clear; Jericho was theirs. Yet they needed to persist before the promise became a reality. The Lord rewards persistence.

Looking In: Do you believe that God will give you victory over your stronghold? Are you persistent even when victory is not apparent? God is committed to victory. Are you? Are you persistent in prayer?

Looking Out: Are you encouraging a brother to be persistent in his battles? Are you pointing to the promises of victory? Are you persistent in your prayers for your brother?

> I see what you've done, your hard, hard work, your refusal to quit. I know you can't stomach evil, that you weed out apostolic pretenders. I know your persistence, your courage in my cause, that you never wear out.
>
> —Revelation 2:2–3 (MSG)

A disciple is persistent in battling strongholds.

Six: Announce the Victory

> "March around the city once with all the armed men. Do this for six day. **Have seven priests carry trumpets of rams' horns in front of the ark. On the seventh day, march around the city seven times, with the priests blowing the trumpets. When you hear them sound a long blast on the trumpets, have all the people give a loud shout; then the wall of the city will collapse and the people will go up, every man straight in."** ... The seven priests carrying the seven trumpets went forward, marching before the ark of the LORD and **blowing the trumpets.**... The seventh time around, **when the priests sounded the trumpet blast**, Joshua commanded the people, "Shout! For the LORD has given you the city!"
>
> —Joshua 6:3–5, 13, 16 (emphasis added)

The trumpets or shofars (typically rams' horns) were used to call the people to worship, signal victory, herald the coming of a dignitary, and warn the people of danger. The trumpets preceded the ark, announcing the presence of the Lord. In addition, the trumpets were a warning of the impending destruction of Jericho. They also signaled the victory of the Lord over the gods of Jericho and the defeat of the Enemy. The Lord brought destruction on Jericho. It was His victory.

The city was still shut up tight. The walls of the stronghold had not been breached. The priests with the trumpets blew the trumpets each day for seven days.

In our struggles against strongholds, the Lord wants us to announce the victory and then watch the walls come down. Our problem in coming against strongholds is that we want to see the walls come down before we shout the victory.

Looking In: Do you set your mind on victory by reading the psalms or other Scriptures, such as Romans 8? These Scriptures proclaim the Lord's victory. After being intentional in confronting your strongholds, do you proclaim victory before the stronghold is breached?

Looking Out: Who are the men in your sphere of influence who are not receiving rest because of strongholds in their lives? Are you coming along side of them in their battles? Are you sounding the victory? Are you encouraging them to step out in faith and announce the victory?

> It stands to reason, doesn't it, that if the alive-and-present God who raised Jesus from the dead moves into your life, he'll do the same thing in you that he did in Jesus, bringing you alive to himself? When God lives and breathes in you (and he does, as surely as he did in Jesus), you are delivered from that dead life. With his Spirit living in you, your body will be as alive as Christ's! So don't you see that we don't owe this old do-it-yourself life one red cent.
>
> —Romans 8:11–12 (MSG)

A disciple knows that the Lord will bring the victory.

Seven: Take the Initiative

> And he ordered the people, "**Advance!** March around the city, with the armed guard going ahead of the ark of the Lord." When Joshua had spoken to the people, the seven priests carrying **the seven trumpets before the Lord went forward**, blowing their trumpets, and the ark of the Lord's covenant followed them.
>
> —Joshua 6:7–8 (emphasis added)

First were the armed men. This was war. As we advance, we must be armed with the Word. In confronting strongholds, we need to take direction from the Word.

Next were the priests announcing the presence of the Lord, warning the citizens of Jericho, and proclaiming victory. We must be prepared at the outset to declare victory.

Third was the ark. We are to put the Lord in front. The Lord is the one who will lead this battle. We must allow the Lord to do the work in bringing down the stronghold. Unless our strongholds or bondages are removed, we cannot have rest. Surrender is not an option. Surrender takes us out of the game. God will select someone else to carry out His plan.

Taking down strongholds is spiritual warfare. We must be intentional in these battles. The command is "Advance!" We must take the initiative. We must be proactive. We must do battle or surrender. Jericho had to be conquered before the Israelites could receive rest.

A man reported, "I was a drug addict doing cocaine, pot, and drinking. I was raised in a good Christian home but did my own thing for many years. I knew Jesus Christ was the only way, but did not understand how to get close to Him. I cried out to Him one day and He took everything away from me but pot. I struggled with this, but He took this away too. I found out the more I prayed and read and studied His Word, the better life became."

Looking In: What is standing in the way of your effective service? Is it a bondage or addiction such as pornography, alcohol, or drugs? Is it an attitude, habit, or behavior? Have you admitted that you are powerless to defeat it? Have you chosen to get rid of it? Have you taken the initiative? Have you made that decision? Do you know the Scriptures concerning the battle?

Looking Out: Are you prepared to lead a man in the battle against his stronghold(s)? Are you there for him in the battle, encouraging him through the power of the Holy Spirit to bring down the walls of his stronghold?

> With the arrival of Jesus, the Messiah, that fateful dilemma is resolved. Those who enter into Christ's being-here-for-us no longer have to live under a continuous, low-lying black cloud. A new power is in operation. The Spirit of life in Christ, like a strong wind, has magnificently cleared the air, freeing you from a fated lifetime of brutal tyranny at the hands of sin and death.
>
> —Romans 8:1–2 (MSG)

A disciple takes the initiative in the battle against strongholds.

Eight: Live the Call Together

> And he ordered the people, "Advance! March around the city, with the armed guard going ahead of the ark of the Lord."
>
> —Joshua 6:7

The army, the priests, the ark, and the people were all involved in the siege of Jericho. Our tendency, particularly as men, is to go it alone. We can solve it. We do not ask for directions. Scripture urges us to come together in agreement when one of us battles a stronghold. It is not a question of just bringing God into the battle; it is a matter of engaging fellow believers. In doing so, we experience victory together.

Upon leaving a men's retreat, a man reported, "Trust and obey– the problem is in doing it. The disconnection between knowledge and practice is great. The pressure of everyday living puts more stress on me than I realize. And thank you for the conference. God is in control and I am leaving refreshed and energized by what I've heard and shared. I thank God for his salvation." The man was renewed as he came together with other men seeking a deeper relationship with the Lord.

Bill was the only man from his church attending men's retreat. One of the groups at retreat grabbed him and said, "You're with us!" Over the course of the weekend, the man observed and experienced what it was like to be with a band of brothers. When he returned to his church, he told his pastor that the church needed a ministry to men and that he was willing to lead it. Today he is taking careful steps and organizing events aimed at building relationships.

"You use steel to sharpen steel, and one friend sharpens another" (Prov. 27:17 MSG). The spiritual journey is not intended as a solo venture. We are called to do it together.

Looking In: When you face strongholds, do you struggle alone? Do you engage fellow believers in coming against your strongholds? Does pride keep you from sharing your need? Are you too embarrassed to bring others into the battle? Do you operate under the mistaken impression that you can fix it alone?

Looking Out: Are you actively engaged with others who are battling sin? Are you encouraging your men to come together against the stronghold a brother may be facing?

> After this the LORD appointed seventy-two others and sent them on ahead of him, two by two, into every town and place where he himself was about to go … The seventy-two returned with joy, saying, "LORD, even the demons are subject to us in your name!"
>
> —Luke 10:1, 17 (ESV)

A disciple encourages the unity of believers in advancing Christ's kingdom.

Nine: Destroy What the Lord Says to Destroy

> And the city and all that is within it shall be devoted to the LORD for destruction.... **But you, keep yourselves from the things devoted to destruction, lest when you have devoted them you take any of the devoted things and make the camp of Israel a thing for destruction and bring trouble upon it....** Then they devoted all in the city to destruction, both men and women, young and old, oxen, sheep, and donkeys, with the edge of the sword.... Then they burned the whole city and everything in it.
>
> —Joshua 6:17–18, 21, 24 (ESV) emphasis added

The word "devoted" means "to set aside." In this case, Jericho was set aside for destruction. Israel was an instrument of God's wrath against the Canaanites. The people of Jericho feared the God of Israel. With the exception of Rahab, all the inhabitants of Jericho failed to place their trust in Him. Moreover, the Canaanites were totally depraved. Their behavior was an abomination to the Lord; therefore, there was total destruction of the wall. It was not breached in several places, but a total collapse of the wall.

Furthermore, by eliminating everything as God commanded, the Israelites would not be tempted to fall into the pagan and depraved practices of the Canaanites.

Addictions and bondage are behavior patterns completely outside of the will of God. They must be eliminated. Purification must be thorough. The Lord's command and His warning foretell what will ultimately happen to all those who reject God and do what is right in their own eyes. Those commands were not just for the Canaanites. The Lord's command is to eliminate everything associated with our bondage and addictions.

Looking In: Do you still have artifacts left over from your defeated stronghold? Have you thoroughly cleaned house? Have you asked the Lord to reveal items in your life that need to be "devoted to the Lord for destruction?"

Looking Out: Are you encouraging the men around you to evaluate their lives to see if any vestiges of their former life are left? Are you making this a matter of accountability?

> Do not be deceived: God cannot be mocked. A man reaps what he sows. The one who sows to please his sinful nature, from that nature will reap destruction; the one who sows to please the Spirit, from the Spirit will reap eternal life.
>
> —Galatians 6:7–8

A disciple strives for purity.

Ten: Be Thorough

> Then they burned the whole city and everything in it …
>
> —Joshua 6:24

There were two phases of destruction: the collapse of the walls and the burning of the city. The Lord brought the walls down. He broke through the barriers. The people burned the city.

The Lord brings the victory, but we need to carry through to eliminate the remnants of the stronghold. Get rid of those elements of the past life that are interfering with our relationship with the Lord and the effectiveness of our service to Him.

While on military assignment in Taiwan, I purchased two beautiful, carved teak temple dogs. They were smaller versions of larger stone dogs positioned outside Buddhist and Taoist temples. As I matured in my faith, I became bothered by the fact that the dogs were a part of pagan worship. It took several years before I could bring myself to destroy the beautiful dogs.

Looking In: How thorough are you in eliminating those things that undermine your walk with the Lord? Have you removed those elements that undermine your effectiveness in serving the Lord? Are there things you cherish from the past and cling to? Do you understand the risk they pose for returning to the attitudes and behaviors of the past?

Looking Out: Are you in an accountability relationship? Are you encouraging your men to be thorough in eliminating barriers to effective discipleship?

> So what do we do? Keep on sinning so God can keep on forgiving? I should hope not! If we've left the country where sin is sovereign, how can we still live in our old house there? Or didn't you realize we packed up and left there for good? That is what happened in baptism. When we went under the water, we left the old country of sin behind; when we came up out of the water, we entered into the new country of grace, a new life in a new land!
>
> —Romans 6:1–3, (MSG)

A disciple is thorough in eliminating sin.

Eleven: Give Your Firstfruits to the Lord

> "All the silver and gold and the articles of bronze and iron are sacred to the LORD and must go into his treasury" …

> **but they put the silver and gold and the articles of bronze and iron into the treasury of the Lord's house.**
>
> —Joshua 6:19, 24 (emphasis added)

The Lord wants the firstfruits [Ex. 23:16; Deut. 26:2, 10; Neh. 10:35; and Ezra 47:12]. Jericho was the first of many victories in the Promised Land. The Lord gave them the Promised Land. He gave them the victory at Jericho. He commanded that the things of great value were to go to the Lord. [Later at Ai, the Lord permitted the Israelites to take plunder (8:2).] Since Jericho was an important city, it was no doubt a wealthy city.

The plunder at Jericho may have been riches beyond imagination, but they belonged to the Lord. The Lord requires restraint and responsibility from those He leads into the Promised Land. These were the Lord's instructions to His people, not to pagans. This is the Lord's way. It may not make sense to us, but it is the Lord's plan.

Furthermore, many of the finer things were from pagan rituals. By setting them aside, the Lord was removing things that would tempt Israel to fall into idolatry and apostasy. Therefore, the items were to be removed from common use.

All we have, the Lord has given to us. He expects us to return at least a tithe to him.

Looking In: Are you obedient in following the Lord's instructions? Do you show restraint and responsibility when the Lord blesses you materially? Do you return a portion to Him? Have you established a disciplined pattern of giving? Have you defined what tithes and offerings mean in your life? Do you really understand that all you have comes from the Lord? Do you recognize what He expects you to return to Him? What is your attitude toward what the Lord gives you in terms of time, talents, and treasure?

Looking Out: Do you discuss giving with your men? Do your men give testimonies about the discipline of giving in their lives?

> But just as you excel in everything in faith, in speech, in knowledge, in complete earnestness and in your love for us see that you also excel in this grace of giving.

—2 Corinthians 8:7

A disciple is disciplined in giving.

Twelve: Bring Out Those Who Belong to the Lord

> But Joshua had said to the two men who had spied out the country, "Go into the harlot's house, and from there **bring out the woman and all that she has, as you swore to her**." And the young men who had been spies went in and **brought out Rahab, her father, her mother, her brothers, and all that she had**. So they brought out all her relatives and left them outside the camp of Israel. But they burned the city and all that *was* in it with fire. Only the silver and gold, and the vessels of bronze and iron, they put into the treasury of the house of the LORD. And Joshua spared Rahab the harlot, her father's household, and all that she had. So she dwells in Israel to this day, because she hid the messengers whom Joshua sent to spy out Jericho.
>
> —Joshua 6:22–25 NKJV (emphasis added)

The removal of Rahab and her family before the Israelites burned the city is the third case where the Lord removed believers before He poured out His wrath on apostasy. The first was the removal of Noah and his family before the flood (Gen. 6–7). The second was the removal of Lot and his family before the destruction of Sodom and Gomorrah (Gen. 19).

These passages tell us that God will, in the end, pour out His wrath on immorality and idolatry. He will destroy the wicked. These passages also tell us that He will remove believers before He destroys the wicked.

Consider the fact that Rahab made a covenant with the spies. It was a covenant with them because she was not familiar with the covenant of the Lord. We need to not only bear a burden for the lost but also protect those who are young in their faith. It is important to note that Rahab reached out to her family; she brought them under the covenant.

Are we reaching out to our families to bring them under the covenant?

Looking In: Do you have a burden for the lost? Are you aware that you are responsible for rescuing the lost?

Looking Out: Are you reaching into the community of immorality and idolaters to bring out the lost? Who in your sphere of influence needs to be rescued?

> Suppose one of you has a hundred sheep and loses one of them. Does he not leave the ninety-nine in the open country and go after the lost sheep until he finds it? And when he finds it, he joyfully puts it on his shoulders and goes home. Then he calls his friends and neighbors together and says, 'Rejoice with me; I have found my lost sheep.' I tell you that in the same way there will be more rejoicing in heaven over one sinner who repents than over ninety-nine righteous persons who do not need to repent.
>
> —Luke 15:4–7

A disciple rescues the lost.

Thirteen: Avoid What God Has Cursed

> At that time Joshua pronounced this solemn oath: **Cursed before the LORD is the man who undertakes to rebuild this city, Jericho:**
>
> At the cost of his firstborn son
> will he lay its foundations;
> at the cost of his youngest
> will he set up its gates.
>
> —Joshua 6:26 (emphasis added)

When the Israelites finished crossing the Jordan, Joshua built a monument or memorial to commemorate the crossing. The victory at Jericho was great! The city and everything in it was completely destroyed. The action at Jericho ends with a curse, not a monument.

In reality, however, the rubble of the ancient city was a marker itself. The monuments that Joshua built, stone upon stone, mark great blessings from the Lord. The ruins of Jericho were the result of the tearing down of the walls and buildings of the city. The destroyed city is a testimony to the Lord's wrath. It was a tearing down, not a building up. It was a message to Israel as well as Canaan. God's judgment is final and complete. His wrath stands against those who live in a continuing state of rebellion against Him.

Joshua's curse is against those who seek to restore what the Lord has judged as immoral. It is against what has been destroyed and eliminated.

When the Lord destroys our strongholds, we need to give Him the credit. He did what we could not. Our testimony needs to clearly point back to the rubble of our past and the Lord's power in rescuing and restoring us.

Looking In: Is your former stronghold a matter of the past? Have you attempted to rebuild what the Lord has cursed? Have you allowed the Lord to build a hedge of protection to keep out the attitudes or behaviors that led to the stronghold?

Looking Out: Are you helping your men to make the distinction between what the Lord curses and blesses?

> Whoever believes in him is not condemned, but whoever does not believe stands condemned already because he has not believed in the name of God's one and only Son.
>
> —John 3:18

A disciple avoids that which the Lord curses.

Fourteen: Be Great in God's Eyes

> So the LORD was with Joshua, and his fame spread throughout the land.
>
> —Joshua 6:27

Joshua was the leader. He was set apart, honored, exalted. Leadership takes many forms. We are all called to be disciples. That means we all are called to lead in one form or another. God calls some to great and broad responsibilities. Others are called to singular or more narrowly focused responsibilities. Throughout the history of the church, some disciples are well-known. Others, the great majority were anonymous. Regardless, as disciples our focus is on others. We are all called to lead men to the throne of grace and salvation and on toward the abundant, spirit-filled life.

All of us are given spiritual gifts. All of us are given a grace gift (Rom. 12:5–8). Some are given leadership gifts (Eph. 4:6–10). That means that the Lord is with us. For some there will be fame. Most of us, however, will live quiet lives, empowered by God, serving Him where He plants us.

Joshua achieved greatness because He listened to God and was obedient. Joshua's greatness was a mantle placed by God. Greatness is in the eyes of the Lord.

Looking In: Are you growing where God has planted you? Do you listen to the Lord? Are you in His Word routinely? Do you listen for the Lord in your quiet time? Do you hear what He is saying?

Looking Out: Are you leading others to the throne of grace? Are you encouraging the men around you to make Jesus the Lord of their lives? Are there men in your sphere of influence who have not entered the abundant life? Who among your men is not leading a spirit-filled life?

> Who is wise and understanding among you? Let him show it by his good life, by deeds done in the humility that comes from wisdom. But if you harbor bitter envy and selfish ambition in your hearts, do not boast about it or deny the truth. Such wisdom does not come down from heaven but is earthly, unspiritual, of the devil. For where you have envy and selfish ambition, there you find disorder and every evil practice.
>
> —James 3:13–16

A disciple is called to be great in the eyes of the Lord.

Avoid Willful Disobedience

Do Not Enter Presumptive Sin

> All the silver and gold and the articles of bronze and iron are sacred to the LORD and must go into his treasury … **But the Israelites acted unfaithfully in regard to the devoted things;** Achan son of Carmi, the son of Zimri, the son of Zerah, of the tribe of Judah, took some of them. So the LORD's anger burned against Israel.
>
> —Joshua 6:19; 7:1 (emphasis added)

The Lord was very clear, "All the gold, silver, bronze and iron belongs to me. All the fine things of Jericho shall go into the treasury of the Lord." Achan, however, could not resist the temptation to keep some of the finer things for himself. The sin of presumption is willful disobedience. It is the belief that God's forgiveness becomes a license to sin. It is knowingly going against God's commands. It is placing faith in God's promises rather than in the promise giver, God Himself.

Willful disobedience is a major misstep; it's all around us, even in the church. It is the belief that God wants me to be happy so I can do whatever makes me happy. Among the sins of willful disobedience are adultery, divorce, drug abuse, alcohol abuse, and self-centeredness. It is destructive, not only to the sinner, but also to those around him.

Looking In: Are you in willful disobedience? Are you rationalizing a sin in your life? Are you willing to admit it, confess it, and repent? Are you banking on God's promises and not God Himself? Are you aware of the consequences of willful disobedience?

Looking Out: Is there a man in your sphere of influence who is being willfully disobedient? Do you have an accountability relationship? Are you leading him along the path to restoration? Is he aware of the potential consequences of his actions?

> And again in this passage he said, "They shall not enter my rest." Since therefore it remains for some to enter it, and those who formerly received the good news failed to enter because of disobedience, again he appoints a certain day, Today, saying through David so long afterward, in the words already quoted, "Today, if you hear his voice, do not harden your hearts."
>
> —Hebrews 4:5–6

A disciple is alert to willful disobedience.

Establish a Godly Routine

> Now Joshua sent men from Jericho to Ai, which is near Beth Aven to the east of Bethel, and told them, **"Go up and spy out the region."** So the men went up and spied out Ai. When they returned to Joshua, they said, "Not all the people will have to go up against Ai ... for only a few men are there." So about three thousand men went up; but they were routed by the men of Ai, who killed about thirty-six of them. They chased the Israelites from the city gate as far as the stone quarries and struck them down on the slopes. At this the hearts of the people melted and became like water.
>
> —Joshua 7:2–5 (emphasis added)

There is a pattern here: spying out the land. Moses did it at Kadesh Barnea. Joshua did it at Jericho. Joshua did it again at Ai.

While the spies brought back a very positive report to Joshua, there is no indication that there was any communication between Joshua and the Lord. While this communication was a pattern in the Joshua narrative (Josh. 1:1; 5:13–15; and 6:2ff), but not this time. Neither is it indicated that the Lord had given Ai into their hands. We are not told God gave the children of Israel instructions on how to take Ai. Was Joshua over-confident?

A disciplined Christian life includes a routine of seeking the Lord. It involves knowing God better and gaining insight into His directions.

A man learned to set spiritual goals for his quiet time. He moved from unplanned, haphazard quiet times to intentional, focused quiet times.

Another man changed his morning routine. Instead of having his quiet time after breakfast and the newspaper, he put his time with the Lord first—even before his first cup of coffee. The man later reported that he noticed a marked improvement in his joy and productivity during the day.

Looking In: When you approach obstacles in our life, do you have a godly pattern for tackling them? Do you survey the situation? Do you ask the Lord for guidance and instruction, even though the solution appears easy? Do you make sure that there is nothing in your life that will impede your progress? Do you solidly place each spiritual battle in the hands of the Lord?

Looking Out: Are you encouraging the men around you to establish and keep a godly pattern in their lives? Is there evidence that they are following that pattern? Are there testimonies of regular communication and instructions from the Lord?

> Very early in the morning, while it was still dark, Jesus got up, left the house and went off to a solitary place, where he prayed.
>
> —Mark 1:35

A disciple keeps a holy pattern.

Be Aware of the Broader Consequences of Disobedience

> But the Israelites acted unfaithfully in regard to the devoted things; Achan son of Carmi, the son of Zimri, the son of Zerah, of the tribe of Judah, took some of them. So the Lord's anger burned against Israel … **So about three**

> **thousand men went up; but they were routed by the men of Ai, who killed about thirty-six of them**. They chased the Israelites from the city gate as far as the stone quarries and struck them down on the slopes. At this the hearts of the people melted and became like water.
>
> —Joshua 7:1, 4–5 (emphasis added)

Because of Achan's sin, the army was defeated and thirty-six men died. One man's sin infected the entire operation. We need to be careful who we bring into ministry. Talent and gifts do not overcome disobedience. The Lord wants to advance His kingdom. He seeks a testimony of victory in His church. Sin is a testimony of defeat.

We saw the power of the Lord when Israel crossed over the Jordan and again when He destroyed Jericho. The Lord directed the action and He overcame obstacles. When Joshua and the people were obedient, the Lord showed His power.

Achan was disobedient and God did not demonstrate His power at the first battle of Ai. As a result, there was failure and defeat.

Looking In: Are there things in your life that are blunting the effectiveness of your ministry? Is the Lord revealing sin that needs to be dealt with? Are you looking for sin and disobedience in your life?

Looking Out: Are sin and disobedience among your leadership? Is there an accountability relationship with your leaders? Do you hold each other accountable? Are sin and disobedience in your fellowship? Are you building relationships such that there is trust and respect? Can you gently raise issues of sin and disobedience?

> Let no one deceive you with empty words, for because of such things God's wrath comes on those who are disobedient.
>
> —Ephesians 5:6

A disciple becomes more aware of his sin the closer he is to Christ.

—Ted Roberts

Ask the Right Question

> Then Joshua tore his clothes and fell facedown to the ground before the ark of the LORD, remaining there till evening. The elders of Israel did the same, and sprinkled dust on their heads. And Joshua said, "Ah, Sovereign LORD, why did you ever bring this people across the Jordan to deliver us into the hands of the Amorites to destroy us? If only we had been content to stay on the other side of the Jordan! O LORD, what can I say, now that Israel has been routed by its enemies? The Canaanites and the other people of the country will hear about this and they will surround us and wipe out our name from the earth. **What then will you do for your own great name?**" The LORD said to Joshua, "Stand up! What are you doing down on your face?"
>
> —Joshua 7:6–10 (emphasis added)

Joshua thought that the Lord had abandoned Israel at Ai and that the Canaanites would recognize the Israelites' vulnerability. Isn't Joshua saying, "Lord, You have dishonored your name?" Think about it. In spite of the miracle of the Jordan crossing and the great victory at Jericho, Joshua is saying that it would have been better to have stayed east of the Jordan. "If You are not there for us, who will give testimony to Your greatness, Lord? You have abandoned us." The Lord's reaction to Joshua's prayer indicates that he was again asking the wrong question.

Why do we frequently ask the wrong question? Recall that Joshua asked the commander of the Lord's army the wrong question (Joshua 5:13). Joshua's mind was focused on the battle ahead. So the question was, "Whose side are you on?" This time the army was defeated and the question was, "Why did you do this to yourself, Lord?" Joshua's question was asked out of anguish and stress. God speaks through adversity. Do we seek to understand what He is saying?

Several men were praying together. One of the men asked for prayer for pain in his back. As a teen, the man had been in an auto accident and had broken his leg. The leg was reset but was shorter than the other leg. Even with a lift in his shoe, the short leg put stress on his back. One of the men said he would not pray for healing the back, but instead prayed for the leg. The Lord restored the man's leg! Ask the right question.

Looking In: What is the first question that pops into your mind when you face adversity? Is your response a self-centered, "Why me?" or are you asking the Lord what He is saying through the adversity?

Looking Out: Are the men in your fellowship asking the right question? Are they listening? What is the Lord saying?

> Be assured that from the first day we heard of you, we haven't stopped praying for you, asking God to give you wise minds and spirits attuned to his will, and so acquire a thorough understand-ing of the ways in which God works.
>
> —Colossians 1:9 (MSG)

A disciple asks the right questions.

Take Responsibility

> Then Joshua tore his clothes and fell facedown to the ground before the ark of the LORD, remaining there till evening. The elders of Israel did the same, and sprinkled dust on their heads. And Joshua said, "Ah, Sovereign LORD, why did you ever bring this people across the Jordan to deliver us into the hands of the Amorites to destroy us? If only we had been content to stay on the other side of the Jordan! O LORD, what can I say, now that Israel has been routed by its enemies? The Canaanites and the other people of the country will hear about this and they will surround us and wipe out our name from the earth. **What then will you do for your own great name?" The LORD said to Joshua, "Stand up! What are you doing down on your face?"**
>
> —Joshua 7:6–10 (emphasis added)

God was absent during the first battle at Ai. At least it appeared that way. There was no communication between Joshua and the Lord prior to the battle. There were no instructions or warnings, and Israel was routed. That must have meant that the Lord had let them down. He had abandoned them. It was God's fault.

The very nature of God is that He is present; He is there (*Jehovah Shammah*). Why are we so quick to blame God when we think that He is not present in our trials and tribulations? God permits crises in our lives for many different reasons. Among them, as in this case, is sin. It is not easy to determine what God is saying in the midst of crises or even immediately after. When we think that God is out of the picture, we need to search our hearts for attitudes and behaviors that stand in the way. We need to ask God to reveal those things that may be interfering in our relationship. We need to be ready to take responsibility. We need to make things right.

Looking In: What is your normal response when you feel that God has abandoned you? Do you blame God? Do you accept responsibility? In the midst of a crisis, do you ask, "What are You saying to me? What do I need to do?"

Looking Out: What crisis are you facing in your fellowship? What is the Lord saying in the crisis? Are there sin issues that need to be resolved? Is your fellowship ready to take responsibility when the Lord points to sin?

> If we claim to be without sin, we deceive ourselves and the truth is not in us. If we confess our sins, he is faithful and just and will forgive us our sins and purify us from all unrighteousness. If we claim we have not sinned, we make him out to be a liar and his word has no place in our lives.
>
> —1 John 1:8–10

A disciple takes responsibility for his actions.

Make Things Right

> The LORD said to Joshua, "Stand up! What are you doing down on your face? Israel has sinned; they have violated my covenant, which I commanded them to keep. They have taken some of the devoted things; they have stolen, they have lied, they have put them with their own possessions. That is why the Israelites cannot stand against their enemies; they turn their backs and run because they have been made liable to destruction. **I will not be with you anymore unless you destroy whatever among you is devoted to destruction. "Go, consecrate the people. Tell them, 'Consecrate yourselves in preparation for tomorrow**; for this is what the LORD, the God of Israel, says: That which is devoted is among you, O Israel. You cannot stand against your enemies until you remove it."
>
> —Joshua 7:10–13 (emphasis added)

When Joshua finally went to the Lord, the Lord responded. He said, "I am not the problem. You are. Now get busy and sort it out!" The Lord gave very clear instructions on the finer things of Jericho. Israel (Achan) had disobeyed. Achan's sin impacted Israel and the Lord's reputation.

The Lord is the one who reveals sin in our lives (in the camp). Before that can happen, we need to prepare to meet Him. That means a conscious effort to set aside anything that will distract us from hearing God. That means carving out a "consecrated" time, a time in which we focus on listening to the Lord. We need to allow the Lord to take inventory of the compartments of our lives. We need to let Him identify the things that interfere with our effectiveness in ministry and in our relationships. We even need to identify our hidden faults (Psalm 19:12).

When our actions are inappropriate, they affect others, undermine our testimony, and mar God's reputation. We must set things right by asking God and those we have hurt to forgive us.

Looking In: When your plans do not work, do you stop and ask the Lord, "Is there sin in the camp?" Have I taken for myself things that should be dedicated to the Lord? The Lord has a plan and a purpose for you. Do you take on God's responsibility? Do you set aside (consecrate) a regular time to allow the Lord to shine His light into the dark corners of your life? Do you make such time a matter of routine?

Looking Out: As you lead men to the throne of grace, are you helping your men identify and address the sin in their camp? As you lead men into the Promised Land, are they focusing on making things right? Have you established a bond of trust that enables you to encourage action? Is there accountability?

> Repent, then, and turn to God, so that your sins may be wiped out, that times of refreshing may come from the LORD, and that he may send the Christ, who has been appointed for you—even Jesus.
>
> —Acts 3:19–20

A disciple moves quickly to set things right.

Pull the Thread

> Early the next morning Joshua had Israel come forward by tribes, and Judah was taken. The clans of Judah came forward, and he took the Zerahites. He had the clan of the Zerahites come forward by families, and Zimri was taken. Joshua had his family come forward man by man, and Achan son of Carmi, the son of Zimri, the son of Zerah, of the tribe of Judah, was taken.
>
> —Joshua 7:16–18

Under the Lord's direction, Joshua took a very deliberate approach to find the sin that caused the problem. We need to work through our feelings, the behavior that led to those feelings, the desires that led to the behavior, and the life focus that led to the desires.[4] Sin results from ungodly thoughts at the center of our lives. Sin occurs when the Lord is displaced from the core of our being. When Christ is not central, the distractions of the world, the ungodly desires of the flesh, and the temptations of the devil move in to fill the vacuum.

Looking In: Are you in the habit of asking what or who is at the center of your life in a situation? Is anything crowding out Christ? What is at the center of your thinking? What changes do you need to make to give Christ complete control of your life? What voice are you hearing? To whom are you listening?

Looking Out: Are you encouraging your men to take spiritual inventory? Can they, without hesitation, testify that Christ is at the center of their lives? Are the men in your fellowship moving together to listen only to the Lord?

> You crazy Galatians! Did someone put a hex on you? Have you taken leave of your senses? Something crazy has happened, for it's obvious that you no longer have the crucified Jesus in clear focus in your lives. His sacrifice on the Cross was certainly set before you clearly enough.
>
> —Galatians 3:1 (MSG)

A disciple keeps Christ at the center of his life.

Be Gentle in Confrontation and Accountability

> Then Joshua said to Achan, **"My son, give glory to the Lord, the God of Israel, and give him the praise. Tell me what you have done; do not hide it from me."** Achan replied, "It is true! I have sinned against the Lord, the God of Israel. This is what I have done: When I saw in the plunder a beautiful robe from Babylonia, two hundred shekels of silver and a wedge of gold weighing fifty shekels, I coveted them and took them. They are hidden in the ground inside my tent, with the silver underneath."
>
> —Joshua 7:19–21 (emphasis added)

Joshua focused on the Lord. The people had been consecrated (prepared) and the Lord had narrowed the search to one man. Joshua's greeting is in the name of the Lord. Joshua approached Achan with a fatherly attitude.

The Lord identified Achan as guilty. Clearly, Achan's heart was softened. There was no need for Joshua to accuse Achan. Was it the consecration? Was it Joshua's greeting? Joshua was seeking a confession. When attempting to identify sin, let the Lord do the revealing. At times, a person's guilt is obvious. We need to gently encourage confession.

Looking In: When you need to confront sin, do you undergo spiritual preparation (consecration)? Do you depend on the Lord to lead you in that process?

Looking Out: When confronting sin, do you approach a brother from within a relationship? Do you draw out a response (build a bridge) or do you make an accusation (build a barrier)?

> When you knock on a door, be courteous in your greeting. If they welcome you, be gentle in your conversation. If they don't welcome you, quietly withdraw. Don't make a scene. Shrug your shoulders and be on your way. You can be sure that on Judgment Day they'll be mighty sorry but it's no concern of yours now.
>
> —Matthew 7:12–15 (MSG)

A disciple is gentle in confronting sin.

Recognize Temptation (All that Glitters)

> Achan replied, "It is true! I have sinned against the Lord, the God of Israel. This is what I have done: **When I saw in the plunder a beautiful robe from Babylonia, two hundred shekels of silver and a wedge of gold weighing fifty shekels, I coveted them and took them.** They are hidden in the ground inside my tent, with the

> silver underneath." So Joshua sent messengers, and they ran to the tent, and there it was, hidden in his tent, with the silver underneath.
>
> —Joshua 7:20–22 (emphasis added)

The Lord commanded Israel *not* to take the things that were devoted to Him; they were not to take the first things. He promised destruction to those who disobeyed (Joshua 6:18–19).

Achan stole what belonged to the Lord and hid the items. No amount of confession, repentance, and remorse could save Achan's life. The result of his sin was very public: Israel was defeated and lives were lost. God was angry. In the New Testament, Ananias and Sapphira lied about what they had given (devoted) to the Lord and they died (Acts 5:1–11). The Lord allowed Israel to take the fine things from Jericho, but those things were to be used for His glory. Achan took the things of Ai for himself.

Pastor Bill Hybels races his yacht. Pat Morley races his Porsche. A layman races his motorcycle. All use what the Lord has given them to reach other men with the gospel. What each of these men have, they have devoted to the Lord. Achan, on the other hand, violated God's command. He hid his booty under the floor of his tent. He took what was devoted to the Lord and kept it for himself.

Looking In: Have you reached the point in your spiritual journey where you know the things God wants devoted to Him? What about life itself? Are you devoted to the Lord?

Looking Out: Are you encouraging the man or men you are discipling to see everything they have as from the Lord? Are they aware of the danger in hording what God has given?

> I am saying this for your own good, not to restrict you, but that you may live in a right way in undivided devotion to the LORD.
>
> —1 Corinthians 7:35

A disciple applies the blessings of the Lord in ways that advance Christ's kingdom.

Understand the Effects of Leaven

> So Joshua sent messengers, and they ran to the tent, and there it was, hidden in his tent, with the silver underneath. They took the things from the tent, brought them to Joshua and all the Israelites and spread them out before the LORD. Then Joshua, together with all Israel, took Achan son of Zerah, the silver, the robe, the gold wedge, his sons and daughters, his cattle, donkeys and sheep, his tent and all that he had, to the Valley of Achor. Joshua said, **"Why have you brought this trouble on us?** The LORD will bring trouble on you today." Then all Israel stoned him, and after they had stoned the rest, they burned them.
>
> —Joshua 7:22–25 (emphasis added)

Achan brought trouble to Israel. He also brought trouble to his family. The Lord made a strong statement about Achan's disobedience. Achan, his family, everything he possessed, and the booty he stole were all utterly destroyed.

The Lord held Achan's sin against the entire nation. Because Achan's sin was like leaven in the camp, it had to be eliminated. Leaven can express the effect the gospel has in working out from the heart into one's entire life and eventually the world (Matt. 13:33). However, the metaphor usually refers to negative influences in a person's life and the community.

Looking In: When you do what is right in your own eyes, do you stop to consider the effect your disobedience has on your family and on those around you?

Looking Out: Do your men understand the damage that results when "doing what is right in their own eyes?"

> "Be careful," Jesus said to them. "Be on your guard against the yeast of the Pharisees and Sadducees."
>
> —Matthew 16:6

A disciple understands that a little evil goes long way.

Establish Markers to Past Sin

> **Over Achan they heaped up a large pile of rocks,** which remains to this day. Then the LORD turned from his fierce anger. Therefore that place has been called the Valley of Achor ever since.
>
> —Joshua 7:26 (emphasis added)

The Joshua narrative reports that Israel built a pile of rocks over the remains of Achan, his family, and his possessions. The Lord wanted people to remember Achan's disobedience. The rocks were more than a grave marker. They were a monument to God's judgment and Israel's failure.

God wanted this monument to be a warning to those who followed. There is a great potential for the people to fall away from the Lord and to "do what is right in their own eyes." It starts with one person. Achan sinned, but the Lord held that sin against the entire nation.

Sin enters in insidious ways. It comes when our guard is down. It comes when we are tired or stressed out. It comes when our resistance is down. It comes when we are with the wrong crowd.

While salvation is an event, sanctification is a journey. We will sin. Once we are forgiven and we repent, we need to set markers to our disobedience. We need to place warning signs.

Looking In: Do you post warning signs so that you avoid making the same mistakes again? Do you avoid situations that compromise your values? Do you post a spiritual guard over relationships with female coworkers or friends? Have you devoted all of your life to the Lord, or are there compartments that you keep hidden?

Looking Out: Are you helping the men around you to set markers in their lives as signposts that warn of dangerous places along their spiritual journey? Are you encouraging your men to identify compartments of their lives that have not been devoted to the Lord?

> These are all warning markers—DANGER—in our history books, written down so that we don't repeat their

mistakes. Our positions in the story are parallel—they at the beginning, we at the end—and we are just as capable of messing it up as they were. Don't be so naive and self-confident. You're not exempt. You could fall flat on your face as easily as anyone else. Forget about self-confidence; it's useless. Cultivate God-confidence.

—1 Corinthians 10:11–12 (MSG)

A disciple posts warning signs in order to avoid repeating past mistakes.

Seek Restoration and Victory

Fear Not

> Then the LORD said to Joshua, **"Do not be afraid; do not be discouraged.** Take the whole army with you, and go up and attack Ai. For I have delivered into your hands the king of Ai, his people, his city and his land. You shall do to Ai and its king as you did to Jericho and its king, except that you may carry off their plunder and livestock for yourselves. Set an ambush behind the city."
>
> —Joshua 8:1–2 (emphasis added)

Defeat brings discouragement. The Lord wants us to get back in the mix. He wants us to go at it again. Achan's sin caused a breakdown in communication with the Lord. Once Israel dealt with that sin, they were again on speaking terms with the Lord. He was again giving instructions. More importantly, He told them they would be victorious. It was not a promise; rather, it was a statement of fact. This time the Lord would be in the battle and they would win. When we have an open channel of communication with the Lord, He will give encouragement, strength, and a strategy. When the Lord calls us to ministry, He is committed to victory. We need to be in tune with Him, His plan, and His timing, and operate under His power.

Looking In: How well connected are you with the Lord? What is in your life that is a barrier to that connection? After failure, are you ready to move forward again? Are you afraid to advance, or have you put fear behind you?

Looking Out: When a man slips and falls, are you quick to come alongside him and encourage him to get back in stride? Are you there to bring him back on the team? Are you prepared to take him through the steps of restoration and renewal?

> Be on your guard; stand firm in the faith; be courageous; be strong.
>
> —1 Corinthians 16:13

A disciple seeks restoration and renewal and rejoins the battle without fear.

Muster Everything You Have

> Then the LORD said to Joshua, Do not be afraid; do not be discouraged. **Take the whole army with you, and go up and attack Ai**.
>
> For I have delivered into your hands the king of Ai, his people, his city and his land. You shall do to Ai and its king as you did to Jericho and its king …
>
> —Joshua 8:1–2 (emphasis added)

In the first battle, Joshua took a limited force against Ai. Now that communication with the Lord was restored, the Lord told him to take the entire army. In the first battle, Joshua misjudged the enemy. He advanced with what he thought, in his own wisdom, was a sufficient force.

We often forget that the battle is the Lord's. We advance on the basis of our own wisdom and strength. When we do that, we tend not to bring everything into the battle that is at our disposal. The battle is the Lord's, and He will provide the wisdom and strength tailored to each situation.

Looking In: When you face difficult situations, when you face the Enemy, do you muster all that the Lord has given you? Do you understand that your battles are spiritual, and therefore, must be dealt with in the power of the Holy Spirit?

Looking Out: Are your men advancing with everything available to them? Are they bringing brothers into the battle with them? Are they engaging the Enemy on their own? Are you encouraging them to advance together?

> And pray in the Spirit on all occasions with all kinds of prayers and requests. With this in mind, be alert and always keep on praying for all the LORD's saints.
>
> —Ephesians 6:18

A disciple brings everything at his disposal into battle.

Claim Victory

> Then the LORD said to Joshua, Do not be afraid; do not be discouraged. Take the whole army with you, and go up and attack Ai. **For I have delivered into your hands the king of Ai, his people, his city and his land.** You shall do to Ai and its king as you did to Jericho and its king …
>
> —Joshua 8:1–2 (emphasis added)

Again, as at Jericho, the Lord told Joshua the enemy had already been defeated. Yet the army had not been formed.

The Lord is committed to victory over sin and death. He is committed to us and to our success in the battles of life. He is committed to us because we are His children. He sacrificed His son to bring us under the cover of righteousness. We are His. He is committed to us as a father is committed to His children. He has won the battle in spite of appearances to the contrary!

Looking In: Do you understand that the Lord is committed to your victory and that He has already given you success? When going into battle, do you see victory as past tense or do you wait until the battle is over? "The righteous will live by his faith" (Hab. 2:4).

Looking Out: Do the men in your sphere of influence understand that the battle has been won? Have they moved from assurance of salvation to experiencing victory over issues and challenges in their lives. Do they understand that, unlike salvation, sanctification is a journey and the Lord is giving victory?

> But Jesus was matter-of-fact, "Yes—and if you embrace this kingdom life and don't doubt God, you'll not only do minor feats like I did to the fig tree, but also triumph over huge obstacles. This mountain, for instance, you'll tell, 'Go jump in the lake,' and it will jump. Absolutely everything, ranging from small to large, as you make it a part of your believing prayer, gets included as you lay hold of God."
>
> —Matthew 22:21–22 (MSG)

A disciple enters the battle claiming victory.

Believe that the Lord Will Provide

> "… you may carry off their plunder and livestock for yourselves."
>
> —Joshua 8:2

Having set aside the devoted things, the Lord then allowed Israel to gather things they would need in the Promised Land. It is a matter of obedience: leaving what the Lord says to leave, and taking what He says to take. Now that they had given to the Lord what He commanded, the Lord was ready to provide for their needs in the Promised Land.

In the second battle of Ai, the Lord not only provided victory; he provided necessities for living. In the course of our walk with the Lord, we need to trust that He will provide as He did for Israel. In our worldly thinking we get things reversed. We give God the leftovers. What happens when there are no leftovers? The principle is to give to the Lord off of the top, the firstfruits.

We need to believe that the Lord will provide: *Jehovah Jireh.*

A man gave his sister money to get her through a tight situation. Several years later the man had unexpected car repairs and had to dip into his vacation funds to cover the expense. His sister called to say that she was reimbursing him the funds he had sent her. The amount covered the cost of the repairs and replenished the vacation account.

A man directing hurricane relief work needed several steel doors of a specific dimension. There were no funds with which to buy them but the work needed to proceed. He went to his knees laying the need before the Lord. An hour later a truck pulled up. The driver stated that he was on his way to the dump to dispose of some doors and thought maybe the relief team could use them. The doors met the need exactly.

The Lord is the Lord of "just-in-time."

Looking In: What kind of adjustments do you make when you think what you have is not sufficient? Are you tempted to dip into what the Lord expects you to return to Him? "Well, it's just a loan. I'll pay it back." Really? Are you that disciplined? More importantly, do you really trust that the Lord will provide?

Looking Out: Are you encouraging the men around you to trust the Lord to provide victory and the necessities for life? Is faith a matter of discussion? Do your men share testimonies about the Lord's provision?

> And my God will meet all your needs according to his glorious riches in Christ Jesus.
>
> —Philippians 4:19

A disciple trusts the Lord to meet his needs.

Follow Orders

> So Joshua and the whole army moved out to attack Ai. He chose thirty thousand of his best fighting men and sent them out at night with these orders, "Listen carefully. You are to set an ambush behind the city. Don't go very far from it. All of you be on the alert. I and all those with me will advance on the city, and when the men come out against us, as they did before, we will flee from them.

> They will pursue us until we have lured them away from the city, for they will say, 'They are running away from us as they did before.' So when we flee from them, you are to rise up from ambush and take the city. The LORD your God will give it into your hand. When you have taken the city, set it on fire. **Do what the LORD has commanded. See to it; you have my orders."**
>
> —Joshua 8:3–8 (emphasis added)

God is a God of detail. Just consider His creation. Consider His instructions for building the tabernacle, its contents (Ex. 25-27), and the temple (1 Kings 6). He has detailed plans for us, plans to prosper us and give us hope and a future (Jer. 29:11). As we mature and gain experience, our natural inclination is to apply what worked in the past to the issues in front of us. The strategy and tactics at Ai were far different from those at Jericho.

Men want to fix things. Do we understand, at the action level, that the Lord wants to fix things more than we do? We must understand that He knows better than we do how to fix things. The Lord has a plan. Ask Him what it is.

Pray for vision and passion to advance Christ's kingdom. Pray for the Lord to provide a plan. Pray for discipline in preparing for and executing the plan.

Looking In: Do you stop and ask, "Lord, what is Your plan for this situation?" Do you pray first? Do you rush in based on what worked in the past? Do you model the process for seeking God's plan: pray first, dialogue, set aside time to consider options, wait on the Lord?

Looking Out: Are you encouraging your men to develop a godly planning pattern for their lives?

> He thought of everything, provided for everything we could possibly need letting us in on the plans he took such delight in making. He set it all out before us in Christ, a long-range plan in which everything would be brought

together and summed up in him, everything in deepest heaven, everything on planet earth.

—Ephesians 1:8–10 (MSG)

A disciple seeks God's plan.

Know Your Role and Responsibilities

> Then Joshua sent them off, **and they went to the place of ambush and lay in wait between Bethel and Ai, to the west of Ai**—but Joshua spent that night with the people. Early the next morning Joshua mustered his men, and he and the leaders of Israel marched before them to Ai. **The entire force that was with him marched up and approached the city and arrived in front of it. They set up camp north of Ai, with the valley between them and the city.** Joshua had taken about five thousand men and set them in ambush between Bethel and Ai, to the west of the city. They had the soldiers take up their positions—all those in the camp to the north of the city and the ambush to the west of it. That night Joshua went into the valley.
>
> —Joshua 8:9–13 (emphasis added)

The plan involved an attack force and an ambush force. The ambush force approached with stealth. The attack force was very visible and confrontational.

When planning to advance Christ's kingdom, we need to bring various spiritual gifts to bear.[5] Some of us move out with a great sense of urgency, without clearly thinking things through. Others of us are more controlled in our approach. A ministry team needs both strategies. A ministry team must be sensitive to the gifts of its members. We need to understand both the benefits and the misunderstandings of the grace gifts.

Notice that each element of the army had a role. In battle, soldiers have different roles and therefore are equipped differently. Paul talks about the different parts of the body needed to function properly (Rom. 12:4–6).

Looking In: Do you know your grace or motivational gift (Rom. 12:6–8)? Are you aware of the responsibilities that go with it?

Looking Out: Do you understand how your grace gift fits with the grace gifts of other members of your team?

> You can easily enough see how this kind of thing works by looking no further than your own body. Your body has many parts—limbs, organs, cells—but no matter how many parts you can name, you're still one body. It's exactly the same with Christ. By means of his one Spirit, we all said good-bye to our partial and piecemeal lives. We each used to independently call our own shots, but then we entered into a large and integrated life in which he has the final say in everything.
>
> —1 Corinthians 12:12–13 (MSG)

A disciple understands his spiritual gifts and how they fit with the gifts of the team.

Be Alert to the Active Enemy

> **When the king of Ai saw this, he and all the men of the city hurried out early in the morning to meet Israel in battle** at a certain place overlooking the Arabah. But he did not know that an ambush had been set against him behind the city. Joshua and all Israel let themselves be driven back before them, and they fled toward the desert. All the men of Ai were called to pursue them, and they pursued Joshua and were lured away from the city. Not a man remained in Ai or Bethel who did not go after Israel. They left the city open and went in pursuit of Israel.
>
> —Joshua 8:14–17 (emphasis added)

At Jericho, the enemy hunkered down. They shut themselves up. Their response to Israel was one of fear (their hearts melted). They were passive.

At Ai, the enemy was active. The army came out of the city and advanced on Israel. Ai responded on offense.

Satan is persistent. When one battle is won, he looks for another avenue of attack. In our spiritual journey, we need to pursue the Enemy and remove him from every corner of our lives. Unfortunately, we are not always thorough in cleaning the corners where the Enemy has camped.

The Lord has a strategy for dealing with passive and active enemies. When we are under attack, we need to be active in our approach. We must be persistent in our prayers. Our battles are spiritual. Jesus taught that in some cases prayer and fasting are required (Mark 9:29). The implication is serious; fervent prayer. Active confrontation may require an army, that is, people, committed to accountability and bearing burdens.

The Enemy attacks with many weapons: depression, despondency, defeat, fear. He comes from many directions: the world, the flesh, and the devil.

Looking in: Do you see the Enemy coming? Do you know the warning signs? Do you take an active approach in confronting the Enemy? Are you meeting the Enemy head on? Are you engaging others in the battle? Are you conscious of the fight you are in? Are you in the fight?

Looking Out: Who among your men are under attack? Where is the Enemy attacking? Do you have a plan of attack? Are your men aware that they are not alone in the battle? Are you in an accountability relationship? Are you making a covenant together against sin in your lives?

> Be self-controlled and alert. Your enemy the devil prowls around like a roaring lion looking for someone to devour. Resist him, standing firm in the faith, because you know that your brothers throughout the world are undergoing the same kind of sufferings.
>
> —1 Peter 5:8–9

A disciple is alert and active in meeting the Enemy.

Understand the Relationship between Obedience and Victory

> Then the Lord said to Joshua, "Hold out toward Ai the javelin that is in your hand, for into your hand I will deliver the city." **So Joshua held out his javelin toward Ai.** As soon as he did this, the men in the ambush rose quickly from their position and rushed forward. They entered the city and captured it and quickly set it on fire.
>
> —Joshua 8:18–19 (emphasis added)

The Lord has a grand scheme, but it is often initiated with the simplest of actions. Take, for example, these commands God has given: "Strike the water" (Ex. 7:17); "Throw wood into the water" (Ex. 15:25); "Strike the rock" (Ex. 17:6); "Speak to the rock" (Num. 20:8); "Step into the water" (Josh. 3:13); and "Give a loud shout" (Josh. 6:5).

Here in our present discussion, Joshua is told, "Hold out your javelin." The Lord initiates action based on the action of men. He wants us to participate in the victory. He has commanded us to advance His kingdom. He wants to work through us. The Lord has a plan; He wants to use us in carrying out that plan. He has placed His Spirit in us to accomplish that plan. We live under God's plan when we are obedient.

Looking In: What is God calling you to do? Where does He want you to start? What is He asking you to do to get started? Are you obeying His instructions?

Looking Out: How do you encourage new believers to step out in faith? Similarly, does your leadership team understand what it means to step out in faith? Are they aware that the Lord will do great things when they step out in faith?

> "I am Jesus, whom you are persecuting," he replied. "Now get up and go into the city, and you will be told what you must do."
>
> —Acts 9:5–6

A disciple steps out in faith.

Rescue the Ready

> The men of Ai looked back and saw the smoke of the city rising against the sky, **but they had no chance to escape in any direction**, for the Israelites who had been fleeing toward the desert had turned back against their pursuers. For when Joshua and all Israel saw that the ambush had taken the city and that smoke was going up from the city, they turned around and attacked the men of Ai. The men of the ambush also came out of the city against them, so that they were caught in the middle, with Israelites on both sides. Israel cut them down, leaving them neither survivors nor fugitives. But they took the king of Ai alive and brought him to Joshua.
>
> —Joshua 8:20–23 (emphasis added)

How many times has the Lord said, "I have already done it"? Yes, we know the rest of the story; Ai was defeated. The king of Ai and his army misjudged Israel, the Lord, and their own strength. The Canaanites knew about the God of Israel, but they failed to transfer their trust from their gods to the Holy One of Israel. They paid the price for that failure. The choice was theirs.

A man received a phone call one morning from a friend with whom he had worked on a church project. The caller stated that his wife had just served him with divorce papers and he needed to talk. They met that morning, and for over two hours went through Scriptures. The man encouraged his friend to go home and discuss what they had just gone through with his wife. The friend called later that afternoon and asked if he could meet with both him and his wife. They met that evening and as a result, both the man and his wife surrendered their lives to the Lord. The divorce was canceled.

Looking In: Have you transferred trust to Jesus Christ? Are you prepared to share the gospel using God's Word? Do you know the Lord desires that all become a part of his kingdom? Do you have faith that the Lord will lead in the sharing of the gospel?

Looking Out: Do you know people in your sphere of influence who are not prepared for the coming of the Lord? Have you built relationships with nonbelievers? Have you warned them that a day will come when they will no longer have a choice? Have you explained that the Lord will come like a thief in the night?

> "How I wish today that you of all people would understand the way to peace. But now it is too late, and peace is hidden from your eyes. Before long your enemies will build ramparts against your walls and encircle you and close in on you from every side. They will crush you into the ground, and your children with you. Your enemies will not leave a single stone in place, because you did not accept your opportunity for salvation."
>
> —Luke 19:42–44 (NLT)

A disciple seeks opportunities to rescue those who are ready to transfer their trust.

Finish the Job

> When Israel had finished killing all the men of Ai in the fields and in the desert where they had chased them, and when every one of them had been put to the sword, all the Israelites returned to Ai and killed those who were in it. Twelve thousand men and women fell that day—all the people of Ai. **For Joshua did not draw back the hand that held out his javelin until he had destroyed all who lived in Ai.** But Israel did carry off for themselves the livestock and plunder of this city, as the LORD had instructed Joshua.
>
> —Joshua 8:24–27 (emphasis added)

Having suffered significant defeat in the first battle for Ai, Israel did not give up. The army pressed forward again. They destroyed the city and all inhabitants. They finished the job. The Enemy has many tentacles. We may achieve what we perceive to be victory and leave openings that allow the Enemy to return—usually with a vengeance (Matt. 12:43–45). When the Lord sets the Enemy on the run, we need His guidance and direction to pursue the enemy and finish the job.

Joshua and Israel finished the job. Saul was told to eliminate the Amalekites, but he did not finish the job and it cost him his kingdom and his life (1 Sam. 15).

Regional leaders in the denomination often report frequent turnover among men's ministry leaders. There is discouragement when success does not happen quickly. Few, if any, men's ministries achieve success in one, two, or three years. *Man in the Mirror* reports that it usually takes at least seven years before ministry to men is effective in discipling men. Persistence is required. In fact, ministry to men is like herding cats. It takes constant time and attention to keep it together and moving forward. Like Joshua, the leadership must continue to hold out the javelin.

Looking In: Do you search for openings that the Enemy can use? What are the situations in your life that lead to temptation? What are the mental paths that lead to inappropriate thoughts that, in turn, lead to inappropriate actions? What about inappropriate images? Do you pursue all avenues open to the Enemy and destroy them? Do you stay with it?

Looking Out: Are you encouraging your men to routinely take inventory? Are they finishing the job? Is there evidence of persistence? Do you hold the javelin for them?

> When a strong man, fully armed, guards his own house, his possessions are safe. But when someone stronger attacks and overpowers him, he takes away the armor in which the man trusted and divides up the spoils.
>
> —Luke 11:21–22

A disciple is thorough and finishes the job.

Mark the Spiritual Victories

> So Joshua burned Ai and made it a permanent heap of ruins, a desolate place to this day. He hung the king of Ai on a tree and left him there until evening. At sunset, Joshua ordered them to take his body from the tree and throw it down at the entrance of the city gate. **And they raised a large pile of rocks over it, which remains to this day.**
>
> —Joshua 8:28–29 (emphasis added)

There was the monument raised following the crossing of the Jordan (4:20). Then there was the monument raised over Achan (7:26) and his family. Now it was time to raise the monument to the victory at Ai. Two markers indicated action by the Lord; one indicated man's disobedience.

Our spiritual journey is filled with victories and defeats. Have we marked those times as lessons learned, whether they are times of dependence on the Lord or times of disobedience? The Lord is saying that we need to do this. We need to stop and reflect on our spiritual journey. Our markers are important in guiding our walk and, through our testimony, becoming a legacy for those who follow.

Looking In: What markers have you posted in your life? Are they physical or mental? Are they journal entries or personal testimonies? Is there one for your salvation? Is there another marking the time you made Jesus the Lord of your life? Are there markers representing other events in your life?

Looking Out: Do your men give testimony to their spiritual victories? Do you give men an opportunity to share what the Lord is doing in their lives?

> But during the night an angel of the Lord opened the doors of the jail and brought them out. "Go, stand in the temple courts," he said, "and tell the people the full message of this new life."
>
> —Acts 5:19–20

A disciple marks spiritual victories in his life.

Celebrate the Victory

> Then Joshua built on Mount Ebal an altar to the LORD, the God of Israel, as Moses the servant of the LORD had commanded the Israelites. He built it according to what is written in the Book of the Law of Moses—an altar of uncut stones, on which no iron tool had been used. **On it they offered to the LORD burnt offerings and sacrificed fellowship offerings.** There, in the presence of the Israelites, Joshua copied on stones the law of Moses, which he had written. All Israel, aliens and citizens alike, with their elders, officials and judges, were standing on both sides of the ark of the covenant of the LORD, facing those who carried it—the priests, who were Levites. Half of the people stood in front of Mount Gerizim and half of them in front of Mount Ebal, as Moses the servant of the LORD had formerly commanded when he gave instructions to bless the people of Israel. Afterward, Joshua read all the words of the law—the blessings and the curses—just as it is written in the Book of the Law. There was not a word of all that Moses had commanded that Joshua did not read to the whole assembly of Israel, including the women and children, and the aliens who lived among them.
>
> —Joshua 8:30–35 (emphasis added)

Because of the mention of aliens, scholars believe that the renewal of the covenant took place after the Gibeonite treaty (Joshua 9). The significant point is stopping to acknowledge God's guidance, provision, blessings, and protection. There was serious effort and intent. The renewal of the covenant had to have taken several days to prepare and several days to carry out.

Looking In: When things go well in your life and in your ministry, do you stop to give God the credit? Do you take time out to thank the One who brought you success? Do you carve out significant time to spend with the Lord in renewing or perhaps even restoring your relationship with the

Holy One? Do you make this a matter of routine in your life? Do you do this in times of trial as well as in times of victory?

Looking Out: Do you guide your men in setting aside times for special thanksgiving and acknowledging what God has been doing in their lives?

> And let your living spill over into thanksgiving.
>
> —Colossians 2:7 (MSG)

A disciple stops to celebrate what God has done and is doing.

See and Hear the Words of the Lord

> There, in the presence of the Israelites, **Joshua copied on stones the law of Moses, which he had written**. All Israel, aliens and citizens alike, with their elders, officials and judges, were standing on both sides of the ark of the covenant of the Lord, facing those who carried it—the priests, who were Levites. Half of the people stood in front of Mount Gerizim and half of them in front of Mount Ebal, as Moses the servant of the Lord had formerly commanded when he gave instructions to bless the people of Israel. Afterward, Joshua read all the words of the law—the blessings and the curses—just as it is written in the Book of the Law. There was not a word of all that Moses had commanded that Joshua did not read to the whole assembly of Israel, including the women and children, and the aliens who lived among them.
>
> —Joshua 8:32–35 (emphasis added)

There are three styles of learning: hearing, seeing, and hands on. The altar was a visual reminder of God's Word. This altar was the fourth monument in the Promised Land. It was created from stones provided by the Lord, not stones carved by man. It was plastered over and the Law carved into the plaster (Deut. 27:2–8). It was another visual reminder to

Israel. This monument, the altar, was a reminder of obedience. The Lord was with Israel, but He expected obedience.

Joshua read the entire law to all of the people. This reading was the audio reminder saying, "We are in this together; all of us." This speaks to accountability. Consider Ezra's reading of the Law on the rebuilding of the walls of Jerusalem. He read the entire law to all the people for revival. Joshua's intent in reading the law to the people was to remind them that keeping the law would preserve the Lord's blessing.

When we hear the Word preached, do we respond individually and corporately? Are we together in our spiritual journey as individuals and as a body of believers? In the exhilaration of victory or success, it is tempting to jump onto the next task. We need to not only give thanks, but we also need to continue to copy the Word of the Lord onto our hearts.

Looking In: What reminders or guardrails do you have in your life to keep you on the path of obedience and victory? Do you have Scriptures that keep you focused? Do you spend daily time in the Word?

Looking Out: Do you encourage your men to keep the Word in front of them? Do you assist the men around you in applying the Word in their lives?

> For everything that was written in the past was written to teach us, so that through endurance and the encouragement of the Scriptures we might have hope.
>
> —Romans 15:4

A disciple stays in the Word.

Be Discerning

Identify Steadfast Fools

> Now when all the kings west of the Jordan heard about these things—those in the hill country, in the western foothills, and along the entire coast of the Great Sea as far as Lebanon (the kings of the Hittites, Amorites, Canaanites, Perizzites, Hivites and Jebusites)—**they came together to make war against Joshua and Israel.**
>
> —Joshua 9:1–2 (emphasis added)

The kings west of the Jordan represent the third of four responses to the army of Israel (God's power—although there is no evidence that they understood that it was God who was defeating the people). The first response was Rahab's, who heard about the God of Israel and made a commitment to the Lord. At the same time, the king and people of Jericho shut themselves up (withdrew) when confronted by Israel. On the other hand, the kings west of the Jordan chose confrontation.

There have always been and always will be those who, together or independently, chose to actively oppose belief in God. This is the Canaanite example. Atheists are active in their denial. The Bible calls them steadfast or committed fools (*nabal*) (Ps. 14:1). They are self-confident, closed-minded, and undeterred in their opposition to God. They seek to draw others into their opposition to God. As believers, we are told to have nothing to do with this type of fool. He will not respond to reason. Our responsibility, therefore, is to live Christ-centered lives in front of them.

Looking In: Have you encountered committed fools? Do you have unavoidable fellowship with committed fools? If this is so, are you careful to avoid areas of conflict (i.e., "shaking the dust from your feet)?"

Looking Out: Do you help your men realize when they have encountered committed fools? Do you assist them in knowing how to avoid committed fools?

> And if anyone will not receive you or listen to your words, shake off the dust from your feet when you leave that house or town.
>
> —Matthew 10:14 (ESV)

A disciple can identify steadfast fools (apostasy).

Do Not Be Deceived

> However, when the people of Gibeon heard what Joshua had done to Jericho and Ai, **they resorted to a ruse:** They went as a delegation whose donkeys were loaded with worn-out sacks and old wineskins, cracked and mended. The men put worn and patched sandals on their feet and wore old clothes. All the bread of their food supply was dry and moldy. Then they went to Joshua in the camp at Gilgal and said to him and the men of Israel, "We have come from a distant country; make a treaty with us."
>
> —Joshua 9:3–6 (emphasis added)

The Gibeonites represent the fourth response to the God of Israel. They chose to make a treaty with Israel. The Gibeonites gave all the evidence of who they said they were. However, as Joshua and the Israelites discovered, they were not who they said they were. They were deceivers. The Gibeonites represent those who infiltrate the body of Christ under false pretenses. They seek salvation by aligning themselves with the community of believers, while hanging on to their own beliefs. Then there are those who sound like believers but hold to heretical teachings such as cults. They give an outward appearance of goodness. They trust that their good works will gain them eternal life.

Clearly, God disapproved of the presence of the Gibeonites. However, Joshua 8:35 indicates that there were aliens present at the renewal of the covenant. Some scholars speculate that they were Gibeonites.

Looking In: Have you made personal alliances with "Gibeonites" in your life? Whom do you allow to infiltrate your space and thoughts?

Looking Out: Are you sure about those with whom you minister? Are they leaving behind the former life? Or are they bringing the culture of the times, or even false teaching into your fellowship? Are there Gibeonites in your fellowship? What are you doing about them?

> These men are blemishes at your love feasts, eating with you without the slightest qualm—shepherds who feed only themselves. They are clouds without rain, blown along by the wind; autumn trees, without fruit and uprooted—twice dead.
>
> —Jude 12

A disciple is careful in entering spiritual alliances.

Be Suspicious

> The men of Israel said to the Hivites, "But perhaps you live near us. How then can we make a treaty with you?" "We are your servants," they said to Joshua. But Joshua asked, "Who are you and where do you come from?" They answered, "Your servants have come from a very distant country because of the fame of the LORD your God…." And our elders and all those living in our country said to us, 'Take provisions for your journey; go and meet them and say to them, "We are your servants; make a treaty with us."' This bread of ours was warm when we packed it at home on the day we left to come to you. But now see how

> dry and moldy it is. And these wineskins that we filled were new, but see how cracked they are. And our clothes and sandals are worn out by the very long journey." **The men of Israel sampled their provisions, but did not inquire of the Lord.** Then Joshua made a treaty of peace with them to let them live, and the leaders of the assembly ratified it by oath. Three days after they made the treaty with the Gibeonites, the Israelites heard that they were neighbors, living near them.
>
> —Joshua 9:7–16 (emphasis added)

Joshua and the leaders of Israel asked the right questions of the Gibeonites, but did not thoroughly investigate their claims or follow through on their suspicions. Clearly the ruse was so elaborate and well thought out that it would have been difficult to learn the truth. However, they did learn the truth later (v16), but that is not the point; they failed to seek the Lord's direction in the first place.

In our ministries, we encounter a lot of ideas. Some do not fit our God-given values, vision, and mission, and should be rejected. Some require evaluation and thorough screening. A few are worth pursuing. In all cases, however, the Lord wants to be our only wise counselor.

A man asked to use our ministry tax-exempt status to solicit corporate donations for a project on which he was working. In return, he offered us name recognition and the potential of a seven-figure income. The project was worthwhile and did not violate any moral standards. The offer was very tempting, except it did not relate to our vision and mission. The man did not deceive us. The deception or distraction was in the money he offered us.

Looking In: Have you been approached to accept an offer that would sidetrack you from your vision or mission?

Looking Out: Do we bathe our plans for our men's ministry in prayer? Do we jump on ideas that, on the surface, look good, or do we give those ideas time for the Lord to speak to their value and effectiveness?

> But now I find that I must write about something else, urging you to defend the faith that God has entrusted once for all time to his holy people. I say this because some ungodly people have wormed their way into your churches, saying that God's marvelous grace allows us to live immoral lives. The condemnation of such people was recorded long ago, for they have denied our only Master and LORD, Jesus Christ.
>
> —Jude 3–4 (NLT)

A disciple is thorough in investigating spiritual relationships.

Do Not Take Solemn Oaths Lightly

> So the Israelites set out and on the third day came to their cities: Gibeon, Kephirah, Beeroth and Kiriath Jearim. **But the Israelites did not attack them, because the leaders of the assembly had sworn an oath to them by the LORD, the God of Israel.** The whole assembly grumbled against the leaders, but all the leaders answered, "We have given them our oath by the LORD, the God of Israel, and we cannot touch them now …"
>
> —Joshua 9:17–26 (emphasis added)

Israel's sin was in not seeking the Lord in the decision about a treaty with the Gibeonites. The elders of Israel would have been within their rights to set aside the treaty because it was based on deception. However, the treaty was made in the name of the Lord. A solemn oath before the Lord could not be broken (Num. 30:2; Matt. 5:33).

A friend of mine promised the Lord that he would become a missionary if the Lord saved his grandmother. The Lord did just that and today, after overcoming a number of obstacles, he is serving on the mission field. Another friend made a commitment to full-time service when he retired, but changed his mind when the time came. Today he suffers from frequent and often debilitating back pain. Is there a connection?

Looking In: Have you made a commitment to the Lord? If not, why not? Are you a disciple? Are you keeping your promise to the Lord?

Looking Out: How well do you screen your men before putting them into positions of spiritual responsibility? Do you assign men duties that do not involve spiritual formation until you can determine the depth and extent of their relationship with the Lord?

> I urge you, brothers, to watch out for those who cause divisions and put obstacles in your way that are contrary to the teaching you have learned. Keep away from them. For such people are not serving our Lord Christ, but their own appetites. By smooth talk and flattery they deceive the minds of naive people.
>
> —Romans 16:17–18

A disciple is discerning in spiritual relationships.

Do Not Compromise

> That day he made the Gibeonites woodcutters and water carriers for the community and for the altar of the Lord at the place the Lord would choose. And that is what they are to this day.
>
> —Joshua 9:27

The record indicates that the Gibeonites were mighty warriors (Josh. 10:2) and that a Gibeonite was a mighty man of David (1 Chron. 12:4). While they called for Israel's help against the western kings, there is no mention of them fighting alongside Israel. Ninety-five Gibeonites helped rebuild the walls of Jerusalem (Neh. 3:7; 7:25).

There is no further reference to Gibeonites as a people except that they lived outside of the camp of Israel (Josh. 10:7).

While the Gibeonites served the Lord in the tabernacle, there is no evidence that they became fully integrated into the life, culture, and worship of Israel. They observed, but remained outside the family of God.

There is no mention of them being circumcised. Did the Gibeonites ever become a part of God's covenant people?

At a personal level, the Gibeonites are compartments that are not fully devoted to the Lord. These are areas of vulnerability. At the corporate level, the Gibeonites are those who align themselves or identify with a body of believers, but are not in reality a part of the family of God.

The Lord issued a warning to Israel. "I will establish your borders from the Red Sea to the Sea of the Philistines, and from the desert to the River. I will hand over to you the people who live in the land and you will drive them out before you. **Do not make a covenant with them or with their gods**. Do not let them live in your land, or they will cause you to sin against me, because the worship of their gods will certainly be a snare to you" (Ex. 23:31–33; emphasis added).

Looking In: Are you aware of compromises in your life? Are you aware of the Enemy's attacks because of those compromises? Are you praying through the compartments that are not fully devoted to the Lord? Are you letting go in those areas, or are you grasping them tightly?

Looking Out: Which men in your fellowship are on the fringe? Who are the ones who believe that being a part of your church will get them into heaven? What steps are you taking to bring those men into the camp?

> Keep yourselves in God's love as you wait for the mercy of our Lord Jesus Christ to bring you to eternal life. Be merciful to those who doubt; snatch others from the fire and save them; to others show mercy, mixed with fear hating even the clothing stained by corrupted flesh.
>
> —Jude 1:21–23

A disciple seeks to bring outsiders into the kingdom of God.

Respond to the Attack

Watch Out for Enemy Attacks on the Fringe

> Now Adoni-Zedek king of Jerusalem heard that Joshua had taken Ai and totally destroyed it, … and that the people of Gibeon had made a treaty of peace with Israel and were living near them. He and his people were very much alarmed at this, because Gibeon was an important city … all its men were good fighters. So Adoni-Zedek king of Jerusalem appealed to Hoham king of Hebron, Piram king of Jarmuth, Japhia king of Lachish and Debir king of Eglon. "Come up and help me attack Gibeon," he said, "because it has made peace with Joshua and the Israelites." Then the five kings of the Amorites … joined forces. **They moved up with all their troops and took up positions against Gibeon and attacked it.**
>
> —Joshua 10:1–5 (emphasis added)

The five kings represent actions or behaviors that steal our peace: a self-help mind-set; stubbornness or failure to submit; self-glorification; and a critical spirit. These sins undermine and destroy the abundant life.

The kings did not attack Israel. The Gibeonites were good warriors and Gibeon was an important city. The enemy needed to eliminate Gibeon before it partnered with Israel as a fighting force.

The Enemy goes after those on the fringe, non-believers and those weak in the faith. Attacks come in the form of destructive or inappropriate behavior, attitudes, ill health, financial issues, job loss, the attraction of the world, or broken relationships. We need to watch out for Enemy attacks.

Looking In: Is the Enemy after you? Can you identify attacks aimed to derail your life?

Looking Out: Do you know of men on the fringe who are under attack? Are you building relationships with them? Are you alert for opportunities to bring Christ into that relationship?

> ... Stand united, singular in vision, contending for people's trust in the Message, the good news, not flinching or dodging in the slightest before the opposition. Your courage and unity will show them what they're up against: defeat for them, victory for you—and both because of God.
>
> —Philippians 1:27–28 (MSG)

A disciple is aware that the Enemy attacks the fringe.

Engage the Enemy Together

> The Gibeonites then sent word to Joshua in the camp at Gilgal, "Do not abandon your servants. **Come up to us quickly and save us! Help us**, because all the Amorite kings from the hill country have joined forces against us."
>
> —Joshua 10:6 (emphasis added)

The Gibeonites were good fighters (Josh. 10:1). The coalition of Amorites was clearly a grave threat or the Gibeonites would not have called for help. In fact, they were desperate.

Desperate situations call for desperate measures. When we are confronted by overwhelming opposition, we need to call for help. That help may be in the form of counsel, or it may be in joining fellow believers who will engage in fervent prayer against the Enemy.

A man sought a job in his community. He engaged his church in praying for a job opening. Unfortunately, there were no openings and he was ready to accept a position in another city. On the day he was going to sign the contract, a local position opened due to an unexpected resignation.

The opening was created when a man woke up one morning stating that God had told him to quit and enter the ministry. Had the man signed the contract, he would have been committed to the other job. We need to engage other believers in our challenges and issues.

Looking In: On a personal level, when you fall victim to an attack because of an area in your life that you have not committed to the Lord, are you bold enough to call for your brothers to engage the Enemy with you?

Looking Out: Do you hear the call for help from those in your midst? Have you taken the time to get to know those on the fringe of your ministry? Get to know them well enough to know when they are under attack. Do you see these situations as opportunities to build bridges that bring those on the fringe into your fellowship and into the family of God?

> Carry each other's burdens, and in this way you will fulfill the law of Christ.
>
> —Galatians 6:2

A disciple does not engage the Enemy alone.

Go Out of Your Way for Others

> **So Joshua marched up from Gilgal with his entire army**, including all the best fighting men. The LORD said to Joshua, "Do not be afraid of them; I have given them into your hand. Not one of them will be able to withstand you." **After an all-night march from Gilgal**, Joshua took them by surprise. The LORD threw them into confusion before Israel, who defeated them in a great victory at Gibeon. Israel pursued them along the road going up to Beth Horon and cut them down all the way to Azekah and Makkedah. As they fled before Israel on the road down from Beth Horon to Azekah, the LORD hurled large hailstones down on them from the sky, and more of them

> died from the hailstones than were killed by the swords of the Israelites.
>
> —Joshua 10:7–11 (emphasis added)

Joshua and the Israelites quickly responded to the Gibeonite plea for help. They were comfortable at Gilgal, but the Gibeonites needed help. Israel responded immediately.

It was twenty-five miles uphill from Gilgal to Gibeon. We can be certain that they carried their weapons and provisions. The situation was desperate. There was no time to think about it. They gathered arms and left immediately—at night.

When the Enemy attacks, he does not come at a convenient time or place.

Looking In: When you (individually or corporately) receive a call for help, how do you respond? Do you delay, waiting for a more convenient time? Do you think someone else will meet the need? Are you willing to go the extra mile, invest time and energy, and go out of your way to meet the needs of those in trouble?

Looking Out: Do you encourage your men to help, to go the extra mile, to go out of their way to meet the needs of other brothers who are in trouble?

> Those of us who are strong and able in the faith need to step in and lend a hand to those who falter, and not just do what is most convenient for us. Strength is for service, not status. Each one of us needs to look after the good of the people around us, asking ourselves, "How can I help?"
>
> —Romans 15:1–2 (MSG)

A disciple goes out of his way to respond to the needs of others.

Respond Quickly to the Needs of Others

> The LORD threw them into confusion before Israel, who defeated them in a great victory at Gibeon. Israel pursued them along the road going up to Beth Horon and cut them down all the way to Azekah and Makkedah.
>
> —Joshua 10:10

At the second battle of Ai, there was a God-given strategy and careful planning, and the Lord brought the victory. At the battle at Gibeon, there was no strategy. The plan was to move out and attack. There was no time to survey or plan. Once again Scripture is clear; the battle belongs to the Lord. He is the one who brings victory.

In our lives, we encounter situations that require spur-of-the-moment response. There may not be time to think when it comes to a sudden death, illness, or other family emergency. The call goes out, "Come quickly."

Looking In: When we deal with an attack by the Enemy, do we just swat at him, chase him away, or do we eliminate him? Have you experienced the Enemy returning?

Looking Out: Are you and your men prepared for emergencies? Do you know who your best fighting men are? Are they prepared to engage the Enemy? Do you have a quick response team or teams with different skill sets?

> If you're called to give aid to people in distress, keep your eyes open and be quick to respond …
>
> —Romans 12:8 (MSG)

A disciple is quick to respond to the needs of others.

Believe in the Lord

> On the day the LORD gave the Amorites over to Israel, **Joshua said to the LORD in the presence of Israel: "O**

> **sun, stand still over Gibeon, O moon, over the Valley of Aijalon."** So the sun stood still, and the moon stopped, till the nation avenged itself on its enemies, as it is written in the Book of Jashar. The sun stopped in the middle of the sky and delayed going down about a full day. There has never been a day like it before or since, a day when the LORD listened to a man. Surely the LORD was fighting for Israel!
>
> —Joshua 10:12–14 (emphasis added)

There is an urban legend that NASA discovered a missing day in computer analysis of the calendar. Others attempt to rationalize the events in the battle. The point is that Joshua prayed for the Lord to intervene in the battle, and the Lord did exactly that! He was directly involved in the victory at Gibeon. He is a hands-on God.

The scenario of God's direct, hands-on involvement has now been repeated four times in the book of Joshua: the crossing of the Jordan, Jericho, Ai, and now Gibeon.

When God commands, He enables. When God directs action, He empowers those involved. He is committed to His people. He is committed to His agenda.

A man was caught up in a period of willful disobedience. It was a significant distraction from the path God had laid out for him. He prayed that the Lord would release him from the power of that disobedience. The Lord broke the bondage and freed him for the ministry to which he had been called. God responds to the prayers of a man. God seeks to advance His kingdom.

Looking In: Do you really understand that God wants to, and will intervene in your spiritual battles? Do you take this personally? Do you really understand that He is committed to victory in your battles or do you struggle on your own?

Looking Out: Are you aware of men around you who are too stressed out to turn the battle over to the Lord? Are you coming alongside them in their battle? Are they aware that you are in the battle with them?

> We have not received the spirit of the world but the Spirit who is from God, that we may understand what God has freely given us.
>
> —1 Corinthians 2:12

A disciple depends on the Lord.

Finish the Job

> Then Joshua returned with all Israel to the camp at Gilgal. Now the five kings had fled and hidden in the cave at Makkedah. When Joshua was told that the five kings had been found hiding in the cave at Makkedah, he said, "Roll large rocks up to the mouth of the cave, and post some men there to guard it. But don't stop! Pursue your enemies, attack them from the rear and don't let them reach their cities, for the Lord your God has given them into your hand." **So Joshua and the Israelites destroyed them completely—almost to a man—but the few who were left reached their fortified cities.** The whole army then returned safely to Joshua in the camp at Makkedah, and no one uttered a word against the Israelites.
>
> —Joshua 10:15–21 (emphasis added)

This would be an encouraging passage except for the caveat "almost to a man." The Enemy is wily. In this narrative, some escaped to fight again another day. So it is when we do battle with the Enemy. We must be thorough in rooting out the vestiges of sin. We cannot leave roots that, like weeds, will grow again. Repentance is a change in direction. It is a stated intention to reverse course in attitude, behavior, or thought.

Looking In: In our confession and repentance, are we thorough in cleaning the compartments where sin resides? Do we stop and take the time to evaluate those things in our lives that will allow an attitude or behavior to recur? Do we truly repent, or do we leave remnants that fester and reestablish the attitude or behavior for which we have just confessed?

Looking Out: Are your men aware of the consequences of not putting their spiritual houses in order? Do you have the kind of relationship with them that permits accountability? Are you transparent? Do you allow them to hear about your own struggles?

> Perseverance must finish its work so that you may be mature and complete, not lacking anything.
>
> —James 1:4

A disciple is thorough in cleaning house.

Believe That the Lord Has Destroyed the Enemy

> Joshua said, "Open the mouth of the cave and bring those five kings out to me." So they brought the five kings out of the cave—the kings of Jerusalem, Hebron, Jarmuth, Lachish and Eglon. When they had brought these kings to Joshua, he summoned all the men of Israel and said to the army commanders who had come with him, "Come here and put your feet on the necks of these kings." So they came forward and placed their feet on their necks. Joshua said to them, "Do not be afraid; do not be discouraged. Be strong and courageous. **This is what the LORD will do to all the enemies you are going to fight."** Then Joshua struck and killed the kings and hung them on five trees, and they were left hanging on the trees until evening. At sunset Joshua gave the order and they took them down from the trees and threw them into the cave where they had been hiding. At the mouth of the cave they placed large rocks, which are there to this day. That day Joshua took Makkedah. He put the city and its king to the sword and totally destroyed everyone in it. He left no survivors. And he did to the king of Makkedah as he had done to the king of Jericho.
>
> —Joshua 10:22–28 (emphasis added)

There is nothing like a visual demonstration. After more than seventy years of walking with the Lord, Joshua's faith continued to shine. The Lord is committed to destroying the Enemy. Joshua was preparing the men of Israel for the battles that lay ahead. The Lord will do it!

This is another R-rated passage in the book of Joshua. It reflects violence at the hand of a man. The narrative tells us that we need to rid our lives of attitudes, behaviors, and thoughts that stand in the way of effective living and ministry. The Enemy is personal; therefore, we need to personally take action to eliminate his inroads. Clearly, we can only do it with the help of the Lord.

Looking In: Have you reached the point in your spiritual journey at which you understand that the Lord will destroy the enemies in your life? Do you understand that He is committed to victory over the enemies you face? Do you have a testimony about victories in your life?

Looking Out: Do the men in your sphere of influence testify about the victories the Lord has brought?

> "I have told you these things, so that in me you may have peace. In this world you will have trouble. But take heart! I have overcome the world."
>
> —John 16:33

A disciple has faith that the battle is the Lord's, and He will be victorious.

Be an Overcomer

Destroy the Enemy in the Power of the Lord

> The LORD also gave [Libnah] and its king into Israel's hand. The city and everyone in it Joshua put to the sword. He left no survivors there. And he did to its king as he had done to the king of Jericho.... The LORD handed Lachish over to Israel, and Joshua took it on the second day. The city and everyone in it he put to the sword, just as he had done to Libnah. Meanwhile, Horam king of Gezer had come up to help Lachish, but Joshua defeated him and his army—until no survivors were left ... They captured [Eglon] that same day and put it to the sword and totally destroyed everyone in it, just as they had done to Lachish ... They took [Hebron] and put it to the sword, together with its king, its villages and everyone in it. They left no survivors. Just as at Eglon, they totally destroyed it and everyone in it ... They took [Debir], its king and its villages, and put them to the sword. Everyone in it they totally destroyed. They left no survivors ... So Joshua subdued the whole region, including the hill country, the Negev, the western foothills and the mountain slopes, together with all their kings. **He left no survivors.**
>
> **He totally destroyed all who breathed, just as the LORD, the God of Israel, had commanded.** Joshua subdued

> them from Kadesh Barnea to Gaza and from the whole region of Goshen to Gibeon. All these kings and their lands Joshua conquered in one campaign, because the LORD, the God of Israel, fought for Israel. Then Joshua returned with all Israel to the camp at Gilgal.
>
> —Joshua 10:30–43 (emphasis added)

Again and again we read that Joshua and the army left no survivors. The repetition indicates that the Lord considered this to be important. As we traverse our own Promised Land, we continually battle the Enemy. We need to lay claim to the Lord's promise to give us victory over sin. We need to be obedient to the Lord's command and leave no survivors.

Looking In: Again, have you permitted the Lord into the dark corners of your life? Have you given Him control and the authority to totally remove the specific sins in your life? Or are you leaving survivors that will rise again to undermine your testimony and dishonor the Lord?

Looking Out: Have you built relationships with your men that include transparency and accountability? Are you and the men around you moving forward against sin in your life and theirs? Are you making it intentional?

> "And these signs will accompany those who believe: In my name they will drive out demons; they will speak in new tongues; they will pick up snakes with their hands; and when they drink deadly poison, it will not hurt them at all; they will place their hands on sick people, and they will get well."
>
> —Mark 16:17–18

A disciple advances against the Enemy in the power of the Lord.

Get the Job Done

> When Jabin king of Hazor heard of this, he sent word to Jobab king of Madon, to the kings of Shimron and Acshaph, and to the northern kings who were in the mountains, in the Arabah south of Kinnereth, in the western foothills and in Naphoth Dor on the west; to the Canaanites in the east and west; to the Amorites, Hittites, Perizzites and Jebusites in the hill country; and to the Hivites below Hermon in the region of Mizpah. They came out with all their troops and a large number of horses and chariots—a huge army, as numerous as the sand on the seashore. All these kings joined forces and made camp together at the Waters of Merom, to fight against Israel … Joshua did to them as the LORD had directed.
>
> —Joshua 11:1–5, 9

In both chapters 10 and 11, there are coalitions of Enemy kings, the encouragement of the Lord, and the obedience of Joshua and the Israelites. The only differences are in the names of the Enemy and the locations of the cities taken. Nine times in chapters 10 and 11 the words "*totally*" or "*completely destroyed*" appear.

The Lord not only gives us victory over death (because of sin), He also gives us victory over sin. He sanctifies us. He is giving us rest in the Promised Land. But that rest does not come without battles against the Enemy. When we experience victory in one area, we are encouraged, but that should not lead us to think that our battles are over.

Looking In: Do you get the point? Do you understand that the Lord is committed to overcoming the Enemy? Do you understand the inroads of the Enemy in your spiritual life? Do you truly know that the Lord will bring the victory?

Looking Out: Are the men around you experiencing victory in their lives? Do they understand the promise of victory?

> Consider him who endured such opposition from sinful men, so that you will not grow weary and lose heart. And you have forgotten that word of encouragement that addresses you as sons: My son, do not make light of the LORD's discipline, and do not lose heart when he rebukes you.
>
> —Hebrews 12:3, 5

A disciple does not stop until the job is done.

Fear Not

> The LORD said to Joshua, **"Do not be afraid of them, because by this time tomorrow I will hand all of them over to Israel, slain.** You are to hamstring their horses and burn their chariots." So Joshua and his whole army came against them suddenly at the Waters of Merom and attacked them, and the LORD gave them into the hand of Israel. They defeated them and pursued them all the way to Greater Sidon, to Misrephoth Maim, and to the Valley of Mizpah on the east, until no survivors were left. Joshua did to them as the LORD had directed: He hamstrung their horses and burned their chariots. At that time Joshua turned back and captured Hazor and put its king to the sword. (Hazor had been the head of all these kingdoms.) Everyone in it they put to the sword. They totally destroyed them, not sparing anything that breathed, and he burned up Hazor itself. Joshua took all these royal cities and their kings and put them to the sword. He totally destroyed them, as Moses the servant of the LORD had commanded.
>
> —Joshua 11:6–12 (emphasis added)

Three times in chapters 10 and 11, we find the sentences, "Do not be afraid" or "Be strong and of good courage." This is one of the most repeated commands in Scripture. As with Joshua and Israel, we are constantly confronted with the Enemy—issues of sin and obedience—and these issues are battles. The Lord tells us to advance and not to be afraid.

Paul said that righteousness comes by faith (Rom. 4:13). It is one thing to hear the message (Rom. 10:17); it is something else to act on the message. Our faith increases as we see the Lord gaining the upper hand in our struggles with the Enemy. The words "Fear not" take on new meaning.

Looking In: What are the challenges you face? Are you seeing progress? Are you being held back by fear?

Looking Out: What evidence do you see among your men that they are being held captive by fear? Do they hesitate in dealing with sin issues? Is there a lack of submission? Are you building bridges to these men? Are you coming alongside them?

> And surely I am with you always, to the very end of the age.
>
> —Matthew 28:20b

A disciple depends on the Lord.

Be Encouraged by Victory

> Joshua took all these royal cities and their kings and put them to the sword.
>
> —Joshua 11:12

Following the defeat at Ai, Joshua and the Israelites proceeded from one victory to the next. They moved through the central region, turned south, and finally headed north, gaining control of nearly all the land. The narrative implies that each victory energized the army for the next battle and victory.

It is a great encouragement to experience the Lord working in our lives. He is always at work. As we look in the rear-view mirror of our lives, we see Him overcoming attitudes, habits, and behaviors. We also see Him working in the lives of those around us through our ministry or just our presence. With each advance, we are encouraged to seek the Lord as we continue to eliminate barriers to sanctification and ministry.

Whether it is dealing with personal sin or barriers to effective ministry, it is encouraging to experience the Lord at work. When we are mired down with personal and ministry struggles, it is easy to be discouraged. That is the point where we need to recommit the issues to the Lord. He will bring victory and eliminate those things that stand in the way of advancing His kingdom.

A man was facing discouragement in an area of ministry to which he believed God had called him. Over a period of six weeks, the man received a number of affirmations that he was where God wanted him in spite of the situation he was experiencing. The Lord encourages us on to victory.

Looking In: When you experience the power of God in your life and victory over a sin, are you encouraged to identify and focus on another area of your life that needs to be brought under the power of the Spirit and the Lordship of Jesus Christ? Have you made a list of the areas, attitudes, and behaviors that lie outside of the will of God? Have you established a discipline of bringing these issues before the Lord for conviction, repentance, and liberation? Does victory in one area encourage you to move intentionally to the next?

Looking Out: Do you encourage the men in your sphere of influence to celebrate victories in their lives and use those victories to focus on another barrier to effective living and ministry? Do you use victory testimonies to energize your men?

> No, in all these things we are more than conquerors through him who loved us.
>
> —Romans 8:37

A disciple is energized by spiritual victories.

Be Thorough

> **Yet [but, however, only] Israel did not burn any of the cities built on their mounds—except Hazor, which Joshua burned.** The Israelites carried off for themselves all the plunder and livestock of these cities, but all the people they put to the sword until they completely destroyed them, not sparing anyone that breathed. As the LORD commanded his servant Moses, so Moses commanded Joshua, and Joshua did it; he left nothing undone of all that the LORD commanded Moses.
>
> —Joshua 11:13–15 (emphasis added)

Perhaps it was a matter of expediency: the pressure to move on to the next battle. By not destroying the cities, they were left unoccupied as the army moved on to conquer other cities. This is a troubling phrase, inserted in the middle of the narrative of Israel's victories. The word "yet" is a coordinating conjunction that indicates an opposite or conflicting idea. Israel conquered kings and destroyed the inhabitants, but failed to destroy the cities.

While Israel conquered the Promised Land, the people continued to struggle against their enemies. As believers, how often do we, with the Lord's help, rout the Enemy; yet leave the places where the sin resided? We are new creatures in the Lord and we should not live in old houses, where sin once resided. This is why Jesus cautioned against pouring new wine into old wineskins.

Looking In: Have you confessed sin and repented? Have you sought out and eliminated the root causes of the sin? Are you aware of the situations that lead to sin: a location or physical place, a hot button issue, exhaustion, stress? What in your life leads to inappropriate attitudes and behavior? Are you burning the cities where sin lived?

Looking Out: Are there men in your group who do not know the difference between confession and repentance? Do you make repentance a topic of discussion among those with whom you associate?

"When an evil spirit comes out of a man, it goes through arid places seeking rest and does not find it. Then it says, 'I will return to the house I left.' When it arrives, it finds the house unoccupied, swept clean and put in order. Then it goes and takes with it seven other spirits more wicked than itself, and they go in and live there. And the final condition of that man is worse than the first. That is how it will be with this wicked generation."

—Matthew 12:43–45

A disciple goes beyond confession to repentance.

Be Persistent

So Joshua took this entire land: the hill country, all the Negev, the whole region of Goshen, the western foothills, the Arabah and the mountains of Israel with their foothills, from Mount Halak, which rises toward Seir, to Baal Gad in the Valley of Lebanon below Mount Hermon. He captured all their kings and struck them down, putting them to death. **Joshua waged war against all these kings for a long time**. Except for the Hivites living in Gibeon, not one city made a treaty of peace with the Israelites, who took them all in battle. For it was the LORD himself who hardened their hearts to wage war against Israel, so that he might destroy them totally, exterminating them without mercy, as the LORD had commanded Moses. At that time Joshua went and destroyed the Anakites from the hill country: from Hebron, Debir and Anab, from all the hill country of Judah, and from all the hill country of Israel. Joshua totally destroyed them and their towns. No Anakites were left in Israelite territory; only in Gaza, Gath and Ashdod did any survive. So Joshua took the entire land, just as the LORD had directed Moses, and he

> gave it as an inheritance to Israel according to their tribal divisions. Then the land had rest from war.
>
> —Joshua 11:16–23 (emphasis added)

Gauging by Caleb's testimony (Josh. 14:10), it was five years between the entry into the Promised Land and the division of the conquered territory.

Chapters 10 and 11 imply a rapid succession of conquests. Actually, these battles took place over a period of at least five years. The Israelites were persistent. They were not in a sitcom where the issues are solved in thirty minutes. They needed spiritual stamina. Spiritual warfare involves a series of battles.

The narrative leads one to believe that these victories were in rapid-fire succession. The narrative describes an intentional process of securing one victory and quickly moving on to the next. The emphasis is on staying in the fight; not giving the Enemy time to recover or prepare for battle. Israel stayed with it until the job was finished.

Looking In: Is there land (sin) yet to be conquered in your life? Is the Lord revealing areas of your life where He needs to work? If not, why not?

Looking Out: Are you encouraging the men around you to persevere in their advance against sin? Are you building relationships that lead to accountability? Are you encouraging men in their walk?

> Therefore, among God's churches we boast about your perseverance and faith in all the persecutions and trials you are enduring.
>
> —2 Thessalonians 1:4

A disciple stays in the fight.

Give Testimony to Victory

Respond to Powerful Challenges

> **Now these are the kings of the land whom the people of Israel defeated and took possession of their land beyond the Jordan toward the sunrise, from the Valley of the Arnon to Mount Hermon, with all the Arabah eastward: Sihon king of the Amorites** who lived at Heshbon and ruled from Aroer, which is on the edge of the Valley of the Arnon, and from the middle of the valley as far as the river Jabbok, the boundary of the Ammonites, that is, half of Gilead, and the Arabah to the Sea of Chinneroth eastward, and in the direction of Beth-jeshimoth, to the Sea of the Arabah, the Salt Sea, southward to the foot of the slopes of Pisgah.
>
> —Joshua 12:1–2 (ESV) (Also, see Num. 21:21–30 and Deut. 2:26–37 (emphasis added)

Chapter 12 summarizes the battles fought by Israel en route to and in conquering the Promised Land. Two kings were defeated under Moses' leadership, and thirty-one kings were defeated under Joshua's leadership.

First, the Israelites encountered Sihon, king of the Ammonites. Moses requested free passage from Sihon; *Sihon* means striking down. Sihon not only refused but also mustered a powerful army to fight Israel. Recall that forty years earlier, Israel refused to move into the Promised Land because they were told that "the people who dwell in the land were strong, and the cities were fortified and very large (Num. 13:28). This time Israel responded to Sihon's power with boldness and confidence, routing Sihon, his sons, and his army.

God's plan always takes us through obstacles that seem impossible to overcome. They seem impossible because they are viewed through human eyes that see the world in terms of human capabilities and limitations. There are always obstacles in ministry.

Looking In: Are you attempting to tackle spiritual challenges in your own strength and wisdom? Do you see your battles through human eyes? When God brings a victory, do you assume that you can apply the same process in your own strength? Are you growing weary in your struggles? Are you doing things in your own strength and wisdom?

Looking Out: Are the men in your sphere of influence seeing victories in their lives? If not, are you encouraging them to deal with their challenges in the strength of the Lord?

> And let us not grow weary of doing good, for in due season we will reap, if we do not give up. So then, as we have opportunity, let us do good to everyone, and especially to those who are of the household of faith.
>
> —Galatians 6:9–10 (ESV)

A disciple overcomes in the power of God.

Overcome Giants

> … and Og king of Bashan, one of the remnant of the **Rephaim**, who lived at Ashtaroth and at Edrei and ruled over Mount Hermon and Salecah and all Bashan to the boundary of the Geshurites and the Maacathites, and over half of Gilead to the boundary of Sihon king of Heshbon. **Moses, the servant of the Lord, and the people of Israel defeated them.** And Moses the servant of the Lord

> gave their land for a possession to the Reubenites and the Gadites and the half-tribe of Manasseh.
>
> —Joshua 12:4–6 (emphasis added)

After Israel defeated Sihon and the Ammonites, Og, the king of Bashan, and his army attacked Israel. *Og* means gigantic. Recall, this is the second obstacle the ten spies reported forty years earlier—the occupants were giants. Fast-forward forty years. God gave the land to Israel and Israel defeated Og and his army.

We frequently face challenges in our lives and ministry that overwhelm us. We do not seem to know where to start. Our frustration leads to feelings of defeat. Encouraging men to seek a deeper relationship with the Lord seems impossible at times. There are times we feel we need a stick of dynamite to get things moving. David faced five giants, starting with Goliath. All were defeated with the Lord's help. We need to look to the Lord in order to defeat the giants in our lives.

Looking In: Do you feel overwhelmed by the size of your challenges? Do you understand, at the action level, that the Lord will bring victory? Do you understand that the Lord will eliminate the Enemy and give you the land?

Looking Out: Are your men facing giants? Are you facing the giant of moving a man, or men, along in their walk with the Lord? Are you advancing in the power of the Lord? Are you encouraging the men around you to advance empowered by the Holy Spirit?

> Beloved, do not believe every spirit, but test the spirits to see whether they are from God, for many false prophets have gone out into the world. By this you know the Spirit of God: every spirit that confesses that Jesus Christ has come in the flesh is from God, and every spirit that does not confess Jesus is not from God. This is the spirit of the antichrist, which you heard was coming and now is in the world already. Little children, you are from God and

> have overcome them, for he who is in you is greater than he who is in the world.
>
> —1 John 4:2–4 (ESV)

A disciple is not overwhelmed by giants.

Give Up Control

> Now these are the kings of the land whom the people of Israel defeated and took possession of their land …
>
> —Joshua 12:1 (Also see Num. 21:21–35; Deut. 2:26–37; 3:1–11)

God's plan was for Israel to enter and conquer Canaan. When Israel refused at Kadesh Barnea, the Lord set aside those who rebelled. Through the next forty years He brought the next generation along with food, protection, and direction as they made their way through the wilderness. He gave them a second chance at Shittim, east of the Jordan. During those forty years the Lord established a culture or mind-set of dependence on the Lord.

Succeeding against Sihon and Og required trust in the Lord. That meant a conscious surrender and submission. For us, like Israel, succeeding against opposition is an issue of power and control. It is the matter of making Christ the Lord of our lives; putting Him in control. For Israel it was geographical. It was a battle for control of the land and freedom of movement. For us, it is spiritual; giving the Lord control and experiencing spiritual freedom. While Moses requested free passage, the Lord's plan was for Israel to occupy the entire land. We often seek free passage through the Enemy's territory when the Lord intends for us to confront the Enemy. Besides, the Enemy will not give us free passage.

The Lord is not satisfied with partial submission. He wants total surrender. Entrance into the Promised Land requires total surrender. Our flesh is a barrier to enjoying the blessings of the abundant life.

Surrender. This is the first issue that we have to deal with before entering into our personal Promised Land. Before achieving rest under the power and authority of the Lord, there must be complete surrender.

Looking In: Have you had a crisis experience? Have you struggled in granting the Lord total and complete control of your life? Can you point to a time or date in your life when you made an intentional and complete surrender of your life and your will to the Lord?

Looking Out: Are there men in your sphere of influence who have not made the step from salvation to submission? Are they aware of the difference? Do you make it a point to share with them the benefits of submission?

> You, however, are not in the flesh but in the Spirit, [since] in fact the Spirit of God dwells in you. Anyone who does not have the Spirit of Christ does not belong to him. But [since] Christ is in you, although the body is dead because of sin, the Spirit is life because of righteousness.
>
> —Romans 8:9–10 ESV

A disciple lives a life surrendered to the Lord.

Remember

> Moses, the servant of the Lord, and the Israelites conquered them. And Moses the servant of the Lord gave their land to the Reubenites, the Gadites and the half-tribe of Manasseh to be their possession.
>
> —Joshua 12:6

The elimination of Sihon and Og and their armies was imprinted on the minds of the people of Israel (and on the minds of the Canaanites). Sihon is mentioned twenty-nine times in the Old Testament and Og twenty-two times. Sihon and Og were the first enemies of many that Israel faced. It was important for the Israelites to keep the victories over Sihon and Og fresh in their memories as they pursued other enemies. The psalmist reflected on these victories brought by the Lord.

> He struck down many nations and killed mighty kings,
> Sihon, king of the Amorites, and Og, king of Bashan …
> —Psalm 135:10–11

Looking In: Do you remember the spiritual victories that the Lord has given you? Do they encourage you in the battles you face now? Do past victories energize you for future battles?

Looking Out: Do you encourage your men to remember the victories the Lord has brought to their lives?

> I write to you, young men, because you are strong, and the word of God lives in you, and you have overcome the evil one.
> —1 John 2:14

A disciple remembers the victories the Lord has brought.

Serve Those Who Lead

> **And these are the kings of the land whom Joshua and the people of Israel defeated** on the west side of the Jordan, from Baal-gad in the Valley of Lebanon to Mount Halak, that rises toward Seir (and Joshua gave their land to the tribes of Israel as a possession according to their allotments, in the hill country, in the lowland, in the Arabah, in the slopes, in the wilderness, and in the Negeb, the land of the Hittites, the Amorites, the Canaanites, the Perizzites, the Hivites, and the Jebusites) … **in all, thirty-one kings.**
> —Joshua 12:7–24 (emphasis added)

Chapter 12 recalls the victories of Moses and Joshua, and the kings they defeated. There was a change of command. The constant was that the Lord brought these victories, not that God honored Moses and Joshua with victories.

It is appropriate to mourn the loss of a leader. However, we should not be discouraged. Discouragement comes when our faith is in the person and not the Lord. When the Lord wants to do something, He will provide a leader, a human leader. The Lord wants to work through men.

Looking In: In whom do you place your faith and trust? Is it a man or is it the Lord? Do you pray for your spiritual leaders?

Looking Out: Are your men aware of the temporary nature of human leadership? Are you pointing out the need to depend first on the Lord as leader, rather than on human leaders? Are you seeking and equipping men who will become future leaders?

> "Therefore it is necessary to choose one of the men who have been with us the whole time the LORD Jesus went in and out among us, beginning from John's baptism to the time when Jesus was taken up from us. For one of these must become a witness with us of his resurrection."
>
> —Acts 1:21–22

A disciple depends on the Lord during changes of human leadership.

the king of Jericho, the king of Ai the king of Jerusalem, the king of Hebron, the king of Jarmuth, the king of Lachish, the king of Eglon, the king of Gezer, the king of Debir, the king of Geder, the king of Hormah,	the king of Arad the king of Libnah, the king of Adullam, the king of Makkedah the king of Bethel the king of Tappuah the king of Hepher the king of Aphek, the king of Lasharon the king of Madon the king of Hazor	the king of Shimron Meron the king of Acshaph the king of Taanach the king of Megiddo the king of Kedesh the king of Jokneam in Carmel the king of Dor (in Naphoth Dor) the king of Goyim in Gilgal, the king of Tirzah

The kings defeated by Joshua

Listen

Hear God's Call
Joshua 13:1–21:45

Find Your Place

> Now these are the areas the Israelites received as an inheritance in the land of Canaan, which Eleazar the priest, Joshua son of Nun and the heads of the tribal clans of Israel allotted to them.... **So the Israelites divided the land, just as the LORD had commanded Moses.**
>
> —Joshua 14:1–5 (emphasis added)

The narrative in chapters 15–19 shows the Lord's plan for the tribes of Israel. He allotted large areas of land to tribes, smaller areas to clans, and fields to families or individuals. With these allotments came the responsibility to subdue and maintain the land. There is great attention to detail in these chapters.

The Lord has specific plans, tasks, or missions for individuals, families, and groups. For example, the Lord gives believers spiritual gifts.[5] He gives them a location in which to apply them. He gives them specific tasks using those gifts. The Great Commission is our mission. We are to make disciples as we go. The Lord has specific Great Commission plans and tasks for each.

As believers, we come together to complete the Great Commission. We are to evangelize, plant churches, equip believers, and encourage disciplemaking. We are to do this in communities, regions, and across the globe. The Lord calls and equips us to advance His kingdom.

Looking In: What is your part of the Great Commission? What has God defined as your territory? What is your mission field? Where are you applying your grace gift and your discipling gifts?

Looking Out: How is your men's group carrying out the Great Commission? How is your family carrying out the Great Commission? Do your men know their God-given territory and their personal mission?

> "But you will receive power when the Holy Spirit has come upon you, and you will be my witnesses in Jerusalem and in all Judea and Samaria, and to the end of the earth."
> —Acts 1:8

A disciple knows where and how the Lord wants him to serve.

Hear God's Call

Begin Anyway

> When Joshua was old and well advanced in years, the LORD said to him, "You are very old, and there are still very large areas of land to be taken over.
>
> "This is the land that remains: …
>
> "… I myself will drive them out from before the people of Israel. Only allot the land to Israel for an inheritance, as I have commanded you. **Now therefore divide this land for an inheritance to the nine tribes and half the tribe of Manasseh."**
>
> —Joshua 13:1, 2, 6–7 (emphasis added)

While there was still land to be possessed, the Lord instructed Joshua to divide both the conquered and unconquered territory among the remaining tribes.

Prior to the allotment of territory, Israel was forced to depend on the Lord in the desert.

Then came five years of war where the Lord brought victory. Dependence or trust was the key to Israel's survival and success. There was still much to be done. However, the Lord instructed Joshua to divide the Land. He did not wait for Israel to finish driving out the Canaanites. We need to clear our personal lives of obstacles that interfere with serving the Lord effectively. However, we cannot wait until we have completed that task. That is a life-long process. We are called to begin serving the

Lord before He has finished refining us. As with Israel, the Lord calls us to begin serving Him in spite of the rough edges.

A man began attending our church at the invitation of a coworker. He had a number of rough personal and spiritual edges. He was discipled by the coworker. Even though he lived twenty miles from church, he began discipling another man, exercised his gift of helps, and was on the outreach team. In the process the Lord began smoothing his rough edges.

Looking In: Are you waiting for the Lord to finish the project—hone your rough edges? Or are you hearing His call on your life and taking action to occupy the territory He has given you?

Looking Out: Are there men in your sphere of influence who need to be encouraged to step out in service? Are you sensitive to areas of ministry for which your men may be equipped, and/or are you paying attention to areas that will get them started in terms of gifting, skills, and talent?

> I do not say that I have already won the race or have already reached perfection. But I am pressing on, striving to lay hold of the prize for which also Christ has laid hold of me.
>
> —Philippians 3:12

A disciple encourages others to serve the Lord.

Separate from Sin and the Ungodly

> **... but they did not utterly drive them out**. Then the people of Joseph spoke to Joshua, saying, "Why have you given me but one lot and one portion as an inheritance, although I am a numerous people, since all along the Lord has blessed me?" And Joshua said to them, "If you are a numerous people, go up by yourselves to the forest, and there clear ground for yourselves in the land of the Perizzites and the Rephaim, since the hill country of Ephraim is too narrow for you." The people of Joseph

> said, "The hill country is not enough for us. Yet all the Canaanites who dwell in the plain have chariots of iron, both those in Beth-shean and its villages and those in the Valley of Jezreel." Then Joshua said to the house of Joseph, to Ephraim and Manasseh, "You are a numerous people and have great power. You shall not have one allotment only, but the hill country shall be yours, for though it is a forest, you shall clear it and possess it to its farthest borders. For **you shall drive out the Canaanites, though they have chariots of iron, and though they are strong."**
>
> —Joshua 17:13–18 (emphasis added)

The narrative in chapters 6 through 12 indicates that the Canaanites were defeated but not driven out. Perhaps Israel's strategy was to remove the Canaanites from the strongholds and then come back and drive out the remaining occupants. However, in verses 15:63; 16:10; 17:13, and 18:3, Israel's failure to drive out the remaining occupants is a disturbing theme. "How long will you put off going in to take possession of the land …?" The implication is that each tribe was capable of driving out the remaining Canaanites in their own territory with the Lord's help. The entire army of Israel was not needed.

There are issues in our lives in which we must engage the Enemy with the entire body of believers. There are other issues that, with the Lord's help, He expects us to conquer. The tribes were satisfied to coexist with the Canaanites contrary to the command of the Lord (Numbers 33:50–53). They were disobedient and suffered the consequences through the ages.

Looking In: Are you complacent? Do you leave vestiges of your old life in place? Are you satisfied to coexist with attitudes and behaviors that undermine your testimony and your witness? Do you separate yourselves from ungodly company?

Looking Out: Do you encourage your men to advance against the enemies in their lives? Is there accountability among your men?

> Since we have these promises, beloved, let us cleanse ourselves from every defilement of body and spirit, bringing holiness to completion in the fear of God.
>
> —2 Corinthians 7:1

A disciple engages those issues that undermine his testimony and dishonor God.

Do Not Fear the Giants

> The people of Joseph said, "The hill country is not enough for us. Yet all the Canaanites who dwell in the plain have chariots of iron, both those in Beth-shean and its villages and those in the Valley of Jezreel." Then Joshua said to the house of Joseph, to Ephraim and Manasseh, "You are a numerous people and have great power. You shall not have one allotment only, but the hill country shall be yours, for though it is a forest, you shall clear it and possess it to its farthest borders. **For you shall drive out the Canaanites, though they have chariots of iron, and though they are strong."**
>
> —Joshua 17:16–18 (emphasis added)

At first, the large tribes of Ephraim and Manasseh argued for more land. Joshua gave them the hill country. But these tribes were also concerned about the Canaanites still living in the land. Their concern about the iron chariots of the Canaanites was the same as the argument forty years earlier that the land was filled with giants. They were saying they could not drive out the better-equipped occupants. Clearly, they had forgotten that with the Lord's help, they had defeated the enemies who had come against them. The issue was not the armies, but the mind-set of the people. Joshua reminded them that they could drive out the Canaanites.

Do we seek more territory, rather than driving out those things that distract us from what God intended? Do we just grow tired of the battle we are in today and move on to a new battle? Does that mean that we are fighting the battle in our own strength?

Clearly, the Lord wants us to renew our minds as we continue on our spiritual journey. That means He expects us to operate in a growing faith that the Lord can and will bring victory in engaging the Enemy. Joshua said that land given to Ephraim and Manasseh was sufficient if they drove out the Canaanites.

A man was discipling two individuals, both of whom were making decisions outside of the will of God. He is learning to depend on prayer and the wisdom of the Lord as he meets strong resistance; however, he wants to keep the doors open in his relationships with each person.

Looking In: Do you hold on to elements of your former life? Do you try to compensate by doubling your efforts, or do you, with the Lord's help, eliminate the sins that interfere with total surrender? The Lord's intention is to clean house. Are you allowing Him to do that?

Looking Out: Do you address head-on the iron chariots in your men's lives? Do your men ask for more "territory" when they have not completed the tasks the Lord has given them?

> Do not be conformed to this world, but be transformed by the renewal of your mind, that by testing you may discern what is the will of God, what is good and acceptable and perfect. (Romans 12:2) As for you, brothers, do not grow weary in doing good.
>
> —2 Thessalonians 3:13 (ESV)

A disciple understands that the Lord can overcome obstacles.

Be Together as One Family

> Then the whole congregation of the people of Israel assembled at Shiloh and set up the tent of meeting there. The land lay subdued before them.
>
> —Joshua 18:1

In the midst of the division of the land, Israel came together. When they established the tent of meeting at Shiloh, the Israelites reaffirmed their unity under one God. They were divided into twelve tribes but were united under one God. Consider parallels between the tribes and the denominations that make up the body of Christ. There are many members of the body of Christ, but only one God.

Consider also that communities of believers are usually made up of several generations. Each generation has a territory consisting of those with similar interests, formational experiences, and age-related challenges. Again, there is diversity in the body but only one God.

Looking In: Do you consider your church as a partner with other churches within your denomination, or churches in other denominations? Do you let theological, culture, or age differences stand in the way of joining others in advancing Christ's kingdom?

Looking Out: Do you work together within the body to convey the message that Jesus is Lord? Do you see the potential for advancing Christ's kingdom together? Do you understand differences among the generations in your church? Do you seek ways to worship and serve together?

> … so we, though many, are one body in Christ, and individually members one of another.
>
> —Romans 12:5

A disciple recognizes the importance of working together to serve the Lord.

Recognize the Challenge of Sin

> So Joshua said to the people of Israel, "How long will you put off going in to take possession of the land, which the Lord, the God of your fathers, has given you?"
>
> —Joshua 18:3

Do you sense Joshua's frustration? The land had been conquered. It had yet to be settled or occupied. Judges 1:1–26 states that the tribes failed to remove the Canaanites. The remainder of the book of Judges relates the disastrous consequences of that failure.

We are confronted by the world, the flesh, and the devil. We can be successful, empowered by the Holy Spirit, in dealing with various sins in our lives. While we may be new men in Christ, the struggle against sin persists. We need to be vigilant; we need to persist.

Looking In: Do you seek to uncover areas of sin in your life and engage, with the Lord, in eliminating them? What are you doing about them?

Looking Out: Do you encourage your men to eliminate areas of disobedience in which their actions, thoughts, and words do not glorify the Lord? Do you stand with them in these battles?

> Likewise, my brothers, you also have died to the law through the body of Christ, so that you may belong to another, to him who has been raised from the dead, in order that we may bear fruit for God. For while we were living in the flesh, our sinful passions, aroused by the law, were at work in our members to bear fruit for death. But now we are released from the law, having died to that which held us captive, so that we serve not under the old written code but in the new life of the Spirit.
>
> —Romans 7:4–6

A disciple persists in eliminating sin.

Understand Where You Belong

> …, and Joshua charged those who went to write the description of the land, saying, "Go up and down in the land and write a description and return to me. And I will cast lots for you here before the LORD in Shiloh." **So the men went and passed up and down in the land**

> **and wrote in a book a description of it by towns in seven divisions.** Then they came to Joshua to the camp at Shiloh and Joshua cast lots for them in Shiloh before the LORD. And there Joshua apportioned the land to the people of Israel, to each his portion.
>
> —Joshua 18:4–10 (emphasis added)

Joshua had allotted the five larger tribes their territory. The next step was to divide the remaining territory among the seven smaller tribes. The issue was finding the right place for the smaller tribes.

Everyone has a place. It is easier to find a place for those who are more obvious in terms of spiritual gifts, talents, skills, and personality. It is more difficult to find a place for those who do not stand out. We need to give special attention to those who stand back or need encouragement.

Looking In: How has the Lord gifted you? Where do you fit in the Lord's plan? Are you called to lead, or be on the support team? What is your role?

Looking Out: Have you surveyed your men? How do you conduct surveys? Is it on paper, by one-on-one conversations over time, or by observation? Do you know the areas where they can serve?

> For as in one body we have many members, and the members do not all have the same function, so we, though many, are one body in Christ, and individually members one of another. Having gifts that differ according to the grace given to us, let us use them …
>
> —Romans 12:4–6

A disciple encourages believers to serve in the right position within the body of Christ.

Understand That Everyone Is Significant

> The second lot came out for Simeon, for the tribe of the people of Simeon, according to their clans, **and their inheritance was in the midst of the inheritance of the people of Judah.** And they had for their inheritance Beersheba, Sheba, Moladah, Hazar-shual, Balah, Ezem, Eltolad, Bethul, Hormah, Ziklag, Beth-marcaboth, Hazar-susah, Beth-lebaoth, and Sharuhen—thirteen cities with their villages; Ain, Rimmon, Ether, and Ashan—four cities with their villages, together with all the villages around these cities as far as Baalath-beer, Ramah of the Negeb. This was the inheritance of the tribe of the people of Simeon according to their clans. The inheritance of the people of Simeon formed part of the territory of the people of Judah. Because the portion of the people of Judah was too large for them, the people of Simeon obtained an inheritance in the midst of their inheritance.
>
> —Joshua 19:1–9 (emphasis added)

The tribe of Simeon was allotted seventeen cities and surrounding villages, not a territory. No boundaries were defined as they had been with the other tribes. The cities and villages were in the Negev. Some believe that Simeon provided a southern buffer across the expanse granted to Judah.

Simeon was a small tribe, but it was given an important function. In the body of Christ, there are organizations that perform important functions in advancing Christ's kingdom; (e.g., the Gideons, a small organization made up of men from many denominations). Because the Gideons are not connected with a denomination, they are able to place Bibles in schools, hospitals, and other areas not open to denominations.

Looking In: What task is the Lord calling you to do? Do you understand the important role that you, as an individual, have in advancing the kingdom? Are you a buffer or an obstacle?

Looking Out: Who in your men's ministry provides a buffer against the enemies that come against your men and your ministry?

> But the LORD is faithful. He will establish you and guard you against the evil one. And we have confidence in the LORD about you, that you are doing and will do the things that we command.
>
> —2 Thessalonians 3:3–4

A disciple is engaged where the Lord plants him.

Recognize the Special Members of God's Family

Finish Strong

> … And Caleb … said to him, " … I was forty years old when Moses the servant of the LORD sent me from Kadesh-barnea to spy out the land, and I brought him word again as it was in my heart.… And now, behold, I am this day eighty-five years old.… my strength now is as my strength was then, for war and for going and coming. So now give me this hill country of which the LORD spoke on that day …" **Then Joshua blessed him, and he gave Hebron to Caleb the son of Jephunneh for an inheritance. Therefore Hebron became the inheritance of Caleb the son of Jephunneh the Kenizzite to this day, because he wholly followed the LORD, the God of Israel.**
>
> —Joshua 14:6–14 (emphasis added)

The distribution of the land west of the Jordan began with Judah. The first to receive an inheritance was Caleb. Caleb reminds Joshua, and the leaders of the tribe of Judah of his faithfulness in following the Lord. He was steadfast in his faith, while the hearts of others melted in fear. Caleb reminds the leaders of his strength and vitality in spite of his age. He was finishing strong. This was Caleb's testimony. It was a powerful statement of faithfulness. Moreover, the land going to Caleb was one of four allotments to individuals mentioned in the Joshua narrative.

The *R* word (retirement) does not appear in Scripture. We are called to persist in ministry to the end. The nature of our ministry may change with age. Regardless, we are called to finish strong.

Throughout the history of the church, there have been those who stand out in their service to the Lord, men who remained strong to the end. There were the disciples, Augustine, Luther, Hudson Taylor, Robert Jaffary, and Billy Graham, to name a few. All stayed the course in advancing Christ's kingdom.

Looking In: Are you keeping the faith? Are you pressing on toward the finish line? Are you remaining strong in the fight?

Looking Out: Are you encouraging the men in your sphere of influence to remain strong in the fight? Are you encouraging them to live in the strength of the Lord? Are you encouraging them to see their battles as the Lord sees them?

> I have fought the good fight, I have finished the race, I have kept the faith. Henceforth there is laid up for me the crown of righteousness, which the LORD, the righteous judge, will award to me on that Day, and not only to me but also to all who have loved his appearing.
>
> —2 Timothy 4:7–8

A disciple remains strong to the end.

Take Responsibility

> And Caleb said, "Whoever strikes Kiriath-sepher and captures it, to him will I give Achsah my daughter as wife." And Othniel the son of Kenaz, the brother of Caleb, captured it. And he gave him Achsah his daughter as wife. When she came to him, she urged him to ask her father for a field. And she got off her donkey, and Caleb said to her, "What do you want?" She said to him, "Give me a blessing. Since you have given me the land of the Negeb,

> give me also springs of water." And he gave her the upper springs and the lower springs.
>
> —Joshua 15:16–19

In Joshua there are four allotments to individuals. The first was to Caleb. The second was to Caleb's daughter, Achsah and her husband Othniel. Achsah, upon her marriage to Othniel, asked him to petition her father for a field. It appears that Othniel did that, but the field did not include a water source. It is uncertain what happened next. Did Othniel fail to recognize the problem or did he not have the courage to approach Caleb again for a source of water? Or was Achsah not content with what she had received? In any case, Achsah approached her father on her own.

Othniel's silence is a lesson for us. We, as husbands, need to step up to our responsibilities in resolving issues and bring spiritual leadership to our families.

Looking In: Do you take responsibility? Do you step up to the plate and do as the Lord asks? Do you see what needs to be done and take the initiative?

Looking Out: Do you have open communication with your wife and children and provide gentle guidance when needed?

> Be on your guard; stand firm in the faith; be men of courage; be strong. Do everything in love.
>
> —1 Corinthians 16:13–14

A disciple is courageous and takes responsibility.

Serve the Disenfranchised

> Now Zelophehad the son of Hepher, son of Gilead, son of Machir, son of Manasseh, had no sons, but only daughters, and these are the names of his daughters: Mahlah, Noah, Hoglah, Milcah, and Tirzah. They approached Eleazar the priest and Joshua the son of Nun and the leaders

> and said, "The LORD commanded Moses to give us an inheritance along with our brothers." **So according to the mouth of the LORD he gave them an inheritance among the brothers of their father.** Thus there fell to Manasseh ten portions, besides the land of Gilead and Bashan, which is on the other side of the Jordan, because the daughters of Manasseh received an inheritance along with his sons. The land of Gilead was allotted to the rest of the people of Manasseh.
>
> —Joshua 17:3–6 (emphasis added)

With the inheritance of the land came provisions for the people. The Lord's instructions in the inheritance covered the disadvantaged. Zelophehad had no male descendents and so there was no allotment of land to his clan. As a result, the Lord made provision for Zelophehad's daughters.

It would appear that Joshua and Eleazar had forgotten Moses' promise to the daughters of Zelophehad. Do we overlook those in need? Do we need to be reminded of our responsibilities to the disadvantaged?

A man, seriously depressed over the loss of his wife, joined the men of his church in making home repairs for a widow in the church. As a result of that connection, the man and the widow began dating and then married. Through the efforts of the men's group, the Lord met the needs of two people.

Looking In: Are you sensitive to the needs of others? Do you get so involved in applying your spiritual gift that you overlook the needs of others?

Looking Out: What are your men doing to meet the needs of the disenfranchised in your midst? Are you intentional in meeting the needs of single women, single mothers, widows, and orphans? Do you carve out an inheritance or allotment for these people? Do you establish their allotment in terms of your time, treasure, talents, and skills?

> "I will not leave you as orphans; I will come to you."
>
> —John 14:18 (ESV)

A disciple seeks ways to help those in need.

Do Not Retire

> When they had finished distributing the several territories of the land as inheritances, the people of Israel gave an inheritance among them to Joshua the son of Nun. **By command of the Lord they gave him the city that he asked, Timnath-serah in the hill country of Ephraim. And he rebuilt the city and settled in it.**
>
> —Joshua 19:49–50 (emphasis added)

Joshua was a faithful servant of the Lord throughout his life. He was a great leader. After the allotment of the land had been made to the tribes of Israel, the people gave Joshua his allotment where he requested. The other allotments had been made by casting lots. That was not the case here. Joshua was given his inheritance from among the inheritance of Ephraim. Scholars point out that Joshua's inheritance was away from the centers of power. His days of leadership were nearing an end. Joshua may have been transferring leadership to the elders of the tribes.

God calls us to serve Him until the end. In Caleb's and Joshua's case, there was a change in focus once the Promised Land had been conquered and allocated to the tribes.

The late Wilmer "Vinegar Bend" Mizell came to know the Lord as a teenager. He was a professional baseball player, three-term congressman, and political appointee in two administrations. Wilmer was an example to me. When traveling on government business, he would call a church in the area he was visiting and offer to speak to their men's group. When asked to speak to secular groups, he shared his testimony. He gave his testimony in both words and actions. He was faithful to the end.

Looking In: What are your plans for retirement? Are you open to changes in your ministry as you advance in years? If you are considering "retirement living," are you also considering "retirement ministry?"

Looking Out: How do you treat those who, at the end of active ministry, move on to the "hill country?" While the Lord provides a heavenly reward for His servants, do you honor them with an earthly reward?

> Whatever you do, work heartily, as for the LORD and not for men, knowing that from the LORD you will receive the inheritance as your reward. You are serving the LORD Christ.
>
> —Colossians 3:23–24

A disciple does not retire.

Be Open, Listen

> Then the LORD said to Joshua, "Say to the people of Israel, **'Appoint the cities of refuge, of which I spoke to you through Moses, that the manslayer who strikes any person without intent or unknowingly may flee there.** They shall be for you a refuge from the avenger of blood. He shall flee to one of these cities and shall stand at the entrance of the gate of the city and explain his case to the elders of that city. Then they shall take him into the city and give him a place, and he shall remain with them. And if the avenger of blood pursues him, they shall not give up the manslayer into his hand …'" So they set apart …
>
> —Joshua 20:1–7 (emphasis added)

The Lord gave Moses specific instructions on providing cities of refuge for those who kill by accident (Num. 35:6–34). The Lord reminded Joshua of those instructions. The Lord's intent is clear: provide a place of protection for those who unintentionally kill another person.

Men often need a place where they can go to get their heads together or deal with anger. They need a place where they are accepted and where they are free to be open and honest. While a refuge may be a physical place, it is more important that they find that place in their relationships with brothers-in-Christ. Men need a place or a person where they can vent their frustrations without being judged.

Several years ago I attended the funeral of my aunt. Before leaving for the funeral, a friend encouraged me to just listen. Following the funeral, I spent the weekend with a cousin and her husband. During that time she poured out her heart to me. I just listened. Hey, I am a guy; I want to fix things. Just listening is out of character for me. At the end of the visit she thanked me profusely for being there. Her husband told me that she had shared things with me that she had not shared with him. People need a safe space and a place to unburden their hearts.

Looking In: Do you have a place where you can go to get your head together? Do you have men in your life who will listen to you as you wrestle with issues in your life?

Looking Out: Do your men have a place of refuge? Do they know to whom they can go to unload? Are you and your leaders transparent? Is there a bond of trust? Do your men have Christ-centered relationships in which they can wrestle with the challenges they face and the bondages that may grip their lives?

> … we who have fled for refuge might have strong encouragement to hold fast to the hope set before us.
>
> —Hebrews 6:18

A disciple is available to listen to others.

Take Care of Your "Priests"

> Now the family heads of the Levites approached Eleazar the priest, Joshua son of Nun, and the heads of the other tribal families of Israel at Shiloh in Canaan and said to them, "The LORD commanded through Moses that you give us towns to live in, with pasturelands for our livestock." **So, as the LORD had commanded, the Israelites gave the Levites the following towns and pasturelands out of their own inheritance: …**
>
> —Joshua 21:1–3 (emphasis added)

In directing the allotment of the land, Moses did not identify any territory for the Levites (Josh. 13:14, 33; 14:4). Once all the territory had been distributed, however, the Levites came to the leaders requesting what Moses had promised them.

The Levites served all the tribes of Israel. Therefore, they were given forty-eight cities and nearby pastureland. These were dispersed among the areas allotted to the other tribes. The Levites' allotment also included the cities of refuge. A major theme in Joshua is that the Lord provides. He provided victory and He provided the land in which they lived. The Lord provided for the Levites.

Besides their temple responsibilities, Levites were teachers, prophets, and spiritual healers. They upheld peace and morality, and according to Malachi 2:4–6, they turned many from sin. They were to be leaven among the other tribes.

As disciples, we are called to be in the world, not of the world. In this sense we are called to be Levites. We are called to minister to believers and nonbelievers. The Lord gifts us as teachers, prophets, healers, and peacemakers. He empowers us to be models of obedience.

Looking In: Do you provide for those who minister in your midst? Is it an intentional act? Do you prayerfully consider supporting Christian ministries outside your church? Are you a Levite within your community of believers? Are you a Levite to nonbelievers?

Looking Out: Who are the "priests" in your men's group? Do they form a holy huddle, or are they scattered among the group? Do they lead small groups? Are they teachers? Do they connect with other brothers for the purpose of evangelizing and discipling? Are they available for counseling and advice?

> … You will do well to send them on their journey in a manner worthy of God. For they have gone out for the sake of the name, accepting nothing from the Gentiles. Therefore we ought to support people like these, that we may be fellow workers for the truth.
>
> —1 John 1:6b–8 (ESV)

A disciple supports Levites in his midst. A disciple is a Levite.

Keep Going

Be Alert to Sin in Your Life. (There Is More to Do!)

> Now Joshua was old and advanced in years, and the LORD said to him, "You are old and advanced in years, and **there remains yet very much land to possess**. This is the land that yet remains …
>
> —Joshua 13:1–2 (emphasis added)

As a continuation of chapter 12, the narrative specifies land that was yet to be possessed. Recall that in chapter 1, the Lord defined the boundaries of the Promised Land. The Israelites had not completed their God-given task; they had not possessed all of the land.

As sons of Adam, there are always more areas of our lives that we need to bring under the control of the Holy Spirit. There is always the continuing issue of who is in control in the various compartments and stages of our lives.

Looking In: Are you aware of the areas of your life that are not under the control of the Spirit? Are you being intentional in turning them over to the Lord?

Looking Out: With whom do you have an accountability relationship? As a matter of routine, do you share about areas that are not under the control of the Lord? Do you use accountability questions? Are members of your group free to hold you accountable?

> "[He] will ignite the kingdom life within you, a fire within you, the Holy Spirit within you, changing you from the inside out. He's going to clean house—make a clean sweep of your lives. He'll place everything true in its proper place before God; everything false he'll put out with the trash to be burned."
>
> —Matthew 3:11–12 (MSG)

A disciple is actively engaged in giving control of his life to the Lord.

Eliminate Sinful Influences

> Yet the people of Israel did not drive out the Geshurites or the Maacathites, but Geshur and Maacath dwell in the midst of Israel to this day.
>
> —Joshua 13:13

Israel did not finish the job. They may have conquered the land, but they did not eliminate the enemy as the Lord had commanded. As a result, the enemy's influence persisted and was a continuing magnet toward disobedience.

Personal Failure. When we are not thorough in cleaning our lives of the unholy, we are tempted to return to inappropriate attitudes and behaviors. They draw us toward disobedience.

Worldly Distractions. We live among people who are committed to disobedience. The world is a powerful influence. The role models in our culture are, all too often, unholy examples.

Looking in: Are you aware of those around you that influence how you think and behave? What influences you today: money, power, position, career, material possessions, substances, entertainment, recreation, talent, fantasy, and religion rather than faith? What leads you astray?

Looking Out: Are you helping the men in your sphere of influence separate the pressure of the world from God's call to obedience? Do you make a habit of discussing the distractions of the world? Is there accountability? Are you working together toward holiness?

> If your right eye causes you to sin, gouge it out and throw it away. It is better for you to lose one part of your body than for your whole body to be thrown into hell. And if your right hand causes you to sin, cut it off and throw it away. It is better for you to lose one part of your body than for your whole body to go into hell.
>
> —Matthew 5:29–30

A disciple is aware of the unholy influences of the world.

Be a Positive Influence for the Lord

> Yet the people of Israel did not drive out the Geshurites or the Maacathites, but Geshur and Maacath dwell in the midst of Israel to this day.
>
> —Joshua 13:13

Israel conquered the land, but they did not eliminate the enemy as the Lord had commanded. In essence, they chose to coexist with the Canaanites. This was an opportunity to advance the kingdom of God among the Geshurites and Maacathites.

We are to be holy examples to the world. We are called to change the world. For most of us that means one person at a time. Jesus told the parable of the sower and the seeds. We need to discern the men whose soil is tillable and fertile (Matt. 13:18–23). Determining the men who are ready involves conversations on spiritual matters. It means being alert to comments that open the door to a spiritual discussion.

I know a man whose wife is a believer. He is not. He has heard the gospel but avoids church. While he is not antagonistic toward the gospel, he is resistant to it. He is hard soil.

A Christian auto mechanic sold a used car to a couple who were not Christians. In rebuilding the engine, he failed to secure a hose clamp. The car overheated, requiring major engine repair. The mechanic did the repairs and refused to accept payment for them. This opened the door to witnessing. Shortly thereafter the couple met with the mechanic's pastor and received Christ. The man's actions created an opportunity with people who represented fertile soil.

Looking in: How much time do you spend with nonbelievers? Do you see opportunities to stand out for Christ?

Looking Out: Do you see men who are open to the gospel, men who need to bring their lives into submission to the Lord? What is your strategy for leading men to the throne of grace and beyond to discipleship? Have you identified people around you who have tillable soil? Are you encouraging your men to seek out these types of people?

> This is good, and pleases God our Savior, who wants all men to be saved and to come to a knowledge of the truth.
> —1 Timothy 2:3–4

A disciple is an influence for the Lord among nonbelievers.

Finish the Job

> But the Jebusites, the inhabitants of Jerusalem**, the people of Judah could not drive out**, so the Jebusites dwell with the people of Judah at Jerusalem to this day**.**
> —Joshua 15:63 (emphasis added)

> However, **they did not drive out the Canaanites** who lived in Gezer, so the Canaanites have lived in the midst of Ephraim to this day but have been made to do forced labor.
> —Joshua 16:10 (emphasis added)

> Yet the people of Manasseh could not take possession of those cities, but the Canaanites persisted in dwelling in that land. Now when the people of Israel grew strong, they

> put the Canaanites to forced labor, **but did not utterly drive them out**.
>
> —Joshua 17:12–13 (emphasis added)

Two of the major themes in Joshua are the Lord bringing the victory and the people's disobedience in failing to follow through and eliminate the pagan occupants of the land. During the five years of battle to occupy the Promised Land, note the increasing frequency of the refrain, "they did not drive them out." What was the problem? Was it a growing weariness with the battle? Was there an unwillingness to pursue the battle to total victory? Perhaps it was comfort and complacency. It was the Lord's command to drive out the Canaanites. The failure was disobedience. The book of Judges and the remaining historical books reveal the consequence of that disobedience; Israel succumbed to pagan influence.

It was recently reported that most of the singles in a large evangelical church were sexually active. A pastor in another church refused to allow a gifted woman who was living with her boyfriend to participate on the worship team. A pastor removed a gifted worship leader from that ministry when the man stated publically that he was bisexual and saw nothing wrong it.

Looking In: Do you grow weary in ministry? Do you let your guard down? Do you fail to pursue the Enemy in your midst?

Looking Out: Are there men in your midst who are not saved or who have not entered into the abundant life? Are they aware of the barriers to spiritual progress in their lives? What are you doing to reach these men?

> As for those who persist in sin, rebuke them in the presence of all, so that the rest may stand in fear.
>
> —1 Timothy 5:20

A disciple is engaged in the battle to clear the land.

Be at Rest

> … And the land had rest from war.
>
> —Joshua 14:15

This statement is a repetition of Joshua 11:23. Why is this statement made when there is more territory to be subdued? Why is this statement made when the historical books recount Israel's continuing battles against their enemies?

The enemies of Israel were subdued. So decisive were the victories that none dared to attack them. There was no peace treaty. It was a peace from, not a peace with (Matthew Henry). For the believer, there will be continuing battles and strife, yet there is rest or peace that comes with knowing that the Lord has brought victory over death and will bring victory over the Enemy. The Lord secures the peace. The Promised Land is far different from the pilgrimage through the desert.

The statements about the land being at rest from war represent the nation and the people becoming conscious of the rest that comes with submission and surrender to the Lord. Rest for the Israelites meant having a permanent place to live. It meant not having to be constantly on the move. It meant having a place to call home.

For us, rest means that the battle for peace with God is over. It means that we are freed from sin and death. It means we understand our place in advancing Christ's kingdom. We know that we have a permanent home in heaven. Our search for God is over. Our life of doubt and questioning is over.

Looking In: Do you have the peace that comes with salvation? Have you seen victories in your life over sin? Have you, with the Lord's help, been able to put behind your attitude and behavior issues? Are you experiencing the abundant or spirit-filled life? Are you at rest? Have you reached the point in your spiritual journey where you know that nothing can come between you and the Lord?

Looking Out: Are the men in your sphere of influence experiencing the rest that comes with the abundant life? Are they moving forward, knowing that the Lord will provide victories over the issues in their lives?

> No, in all these things we are more than conquerors through him who loved us. For I am sure that neither death nor life, nor angels nor rulers, nor things present nor things to come, nor powers, nor height nor depth, nor anything else in all creation, will be able to separate us from the love of God in Christ Jesus our LORD.
>
> —Romans 8:37–39 (ESV)

A disciple rests in the Lord.

Respond

Advance in Obedience
Joshua 22:1–24:33

Serve the Lord

But as for me and my household, we will serve the LORD.
—Joshua 24:15

The Old Testament is about Israel's spiritual journey and our individual spiritual journey. Our spiritual journey begins with God's commitment to us, His mercy in saving us, His leading us on the way, His giving us His spirit, His victories in battling sin, His calling us to ministry, and His releasing us to serve Him.

The last two chapters of Joshua are about being released for ministry. The land had been divided and allotted to the tribes. It was time to settle after five years of battle. It was time to finish the job of removing the original occupants of the land.

In our spiritual journey, we need to acknowledge God's call and begin carrying out the tasks He has given us. In His power, we overcome sin and distractions that hold us back.

A professional Santa Claus always told children the candy-cane story.[6] His boss asked him not to tell the story. He told his employer that he could not and would not be back.

A man was asked by an event hostess to play only secular seasonal songs at a Christmas party. When he replied that his talent came from the Lord and that he could not comply, she relented.

Looking In: Are you responding to God's call? Are you leading your family? Are you leading another man or men on their spiritual journey? Are you willing to serve the Lord at all costs?

Looking Out: Do you have an intentional process for helping your men to hear God's call? Do you have a process for preparing them for ministry?

> … "Worship the Lord your God, and only him. Serve him with absolute single-heartedness."
>
> —Matthew 4:10 (MSG)

A disciple serves the Lord.

Charge to Leaders

Release the Servants

> At that time Joshua summoned the Reubenites and the Gadites and the half-tribe of Manasseh, and said to them, "You have kept all that Moses the servant of the LORD commanded you and have obeyed my voice in all that I have commanded you. You have not forsaken your brothers these many days, down to this day, but have been careful to keep the charge of the LORD your God. And now the LORD your God has given rest to your brothers, as he promised them. **Therefore turn and go to your tents in the land where your possession lies, which Moses the servant of the LORD gave you on the other side of the Jordan.**
>
> —Joshua 22:1–4 (emphasis added)

The eastern tribes had carried out their agreement to help the remaining tribes conquer the Promised Land west of the Jordan River. When they made that commitment, they had no idea how long the job would take. The job was now completed. They were free to return to their allotted lands east of the Jordan. As Joshua stated, they had done well. Joshua was releasing them to a new chapter in their lives.

Ministry often involves partnerships to achieve goals. Various ministries in the church may need to come together to achieve a goal, such as a building program, an outreach ministry, or a community project. At times churches may need to partner in ministry efforts, such as supporting a mission field project, a community soup kitchen, or an evangelistic outreach. When the goal has been achieved, we need to celebrate the achievement and release the partners. For example, at the conclusion of our summer children's Bible Club, the church hosts the workers to express appreciation and celebrate what the Lord did.

Looking In: Are you in the battle for the long term? Are you staying with the challenge? Do you consistently obey those who are your leaders? Do you obey the Lord? What will the Lord say to you when you complete a task or reach the end of this life?

Looking Out: Do you recognize those who have helped achieve a goal? When faithful servants leave, do you acknowledge their contributions?

> "Well done, good and faithful servant. You have been faithful over a little; I will set you over much. Enter into the joy of your master."
>
> —Matthew 25:23 (MSG)

A disciple recognizes faithful service.

Serve Faithfully

> "Only be very careful to observe the commandment and the law that Moses the servant of the LORD commanded you, to love the LORD your God, and to walk in all his ways and to keep his commandments and to cling to him and to serve him with all your heart and with all your soul." So Joshua blessed them and sent them away, and they went to their tents.
>
> —Joshua 22:5–6

As Joshua released the men of the eastern tribes to return to their allotted lands, he exhorted them to be faithful to the Lord.

In ministering to men, our goal needs to be releasing them to service. As they mature in their spiritual journey, we release them to minister in the market place, at home with family, and in church. At the same time, we must challenge them to obedience and hold them accountable.

Looking In: Do you willfully release men to other service once a goal is met in their current position?

Looking Out: Are you consciously aware of the distractions and pitfalls that await the men you are discipling? Do you consistently remember to encourage or exhort them to remain steadfast in the Lord? Is Joshua's statement to these men your benediction when you send your men into life and ministry?

> Blessed is the man who remains steadfast under trial, for when he has stood the test he will receive the crown of life, which God has promised to those who love him.
>
> —James 1:12

A disciple blesses those who are sent out.

Share the Blessings

> Now to the one half of the tribe of Manasseh Moses had given a possession in Bashan, but to the other half Joshua had given a possession beside their brothers in the land west of the Jordan. And when Joshua sent them away to their homes and blessed them, **he said to them, "Go back to your tents with much wealth and with very much livestock, with silver, gold, bronze, and iron, and with much clothing. Divide the spoil of your enemies with your brothers."** So the people of Reuben and the people of Gad and the half-tribe of Manasseh returned home, parting from the people of Israel at Shiloh, which is in the land of Canaan, to go to the land of Gilead, their own land of which they had possessed themselves by command of the LORD through Moses.
>
> —Joshua 22:7–9 (emphasis added)

On releasing the tribes to return to their lands, Joshua instructed them to spread the wealth—the spoils of victory—taken from their enemies. This included clothing, gold, silver, iron, and livestock.

So it is, when God blesses us, we in turn need to bless others. God is always at work and He intends for us to give testimony to what He is doing. The spoils of victory are not always material in nature. We are instructed to encourage one another, to share what the Lord has done, or give a word of knowledge, provide help as needed, etc. (1 Cor. 12:4–11).

Looking In: Do we routinely take inventory of what the Lord is doing? Do we make it a point to share that with family, friends, neighbors, and coworkers? God's blessings are not to be hoarded. They are to be shared.

Looking Out: Do you encourage men to give testimony to what God is doing in their lives?

> But when you proclaim his truth in everyday speech, you're letting others in on the truth so that they can grow and be strong and experience his presence with you.
>
> —2 Corinthians 14:3 (MSG)

A disciple shares God's blessings.

Acknowledge Your Perceptions

Be Alert to Apostasy

> And when they came to the region of the Jordan that is in the land of Canaan, the people of Reuben and the people of Gad and the half-tribe of Manasseh built there an altar by the Jordan, an altar of imposing size. And the people of Israel heard it said, "Behold, the people of Reuben and the people of Gad and the half-tribe of Manasseh have built the altar at the frontier of the land of Canaan, in the region about the Jordan, on the side that belongs to the people of Israel." **And when the people of Israel heard of it, the whole assembly of the people of Israel gathered at Shiloh to make war against them.**
>
> —Joshua 22:10–12 (emphasis added)

The eastern tribes built the altar on the western side of the Jordan, "the frontier of the land of Canaan … on the side that belonged to Israel." It was not clear to the western tribes what their intentions were: competing with the altar at Shechem, or had the eastern tribes strayed from the Lord God of Israel? Whatever it was, Israel was alert to the possibility of apostasy.

I began conversations with a man on our beliefs. After several exchanges, it became apparent that his beliefs were considerably different from mine. Among the showstoppers was his denial that Jesus is God. I began to pull that thread and discovered a number of other significant differences in our beliefs. Scriptural evidence made no impact on him. He remained firm in his convictions. I became convinced that he was, according to Scripture, a committed fool. He was persistent in trying to convince me he was right. He was apostate. Therefore, I severed my relationship with him.

Looking In: Do you recognize apostasy when you see it? Do you distinguish between apostasy and the internal debates of your church? Are you a contrarian? Are you engaged in building bridges or barriers? Do you help keep the focus on the Great Commission?

Looking Out: Do any of your men love to debate the things of God? Do they hold to unorthodox beliefs? Are they persuaded by scriptural evidence? If not, are you prepared to separate them from the other men so as not to poison the growth of the group?

> Many deceivers, who do not acknowledge Jesus Christ as coming in the flesh, have gone out into the world. Any such person is the deceiver and the antichrist. Watch out that you do not lose what you have worked for, but that you may be rewarded fully.
>
> —2 John 1:7–8

A disciple is alert to apostasy.

Be Slow to Judge

> And when the people of Israel heard of it, the whole assembly of the people of Israel gathered at Shiloh to make war against them.
>
> —Joshua 22:12

The western tribes jumped to a conclusion about the new altar. What did it mean? Were the eastern tribes going their own way? The western tribes were willing to go to war over their perceptions. Fortunately, before acting, they sent an imposing delegation to investigate and determine what was really going on.

Patrick Morley tells the story of a man who answered a cell phone in a gym. He put it on speaker. The caller was a woman. She reported that she had found a great leather jacket for one thousand dollars. He told her to go ahead and get it. Then she described a sixty-five thousand dollar vehicle and a million dollar house. The man told her to go ahead and get them. They expressed their love for each other and hung up. The man then asked, "Whose phone is this?"

Things are not always what they seem, particularly in the spiritual realm. When something does not sound right, we need to look before we leap.

How often do we jump to conclusions? There is a lot going on in our lives today. We do not live in simple times. There are pressures at work and at home. We may get stressed out over life. When things do not appear to be going right, we may react inappropriately. We may make bad judgments. Before acting on our perceptions, we need to have a clear understanding about what is happening. Paul exhorts us to test everything (1 Thess. 5:21). Stephen Covey has stated that one should first seek to understand before seeking to be understood.

Looking In: How often do you base your actions on perceptions? Are you patient, and do you make an effort to understand the actions of others, or are you quick to judge? Do you take the time and effort to find the truth? Do you stop and check your filters when you see or hear something that does not seem right?

Looking Out: Do you encourage your men to patiently check things out before they react?

> Know this, my beloved brothers: let every person be quick to hear, slow to speak, slow to anger; for the anger of man does not produce the righteousness that God requires.
>
> —James 1:19–20

A disciple is slow to anger.

Recognize Barriers to Communication

> And when the people of Israel heard of it, the whole assembly of the people of Israel gathered at Shiloh to make war against them.
>
> —Joshua 22:12

There were no cell phones or Internet connections in Joshua's day. The western tribes heard what was happening on the bank of the river, but there was no communication among the tribes. There was distance between them—distance that was a barrier to communication.

Recall the game of gossip in which a message is passed from one person to the next in a circle. It was always humorous to compare the message at the end with the one at the start. Barriers may come in different forms: a noisy environment, age and gender differences, cultural and language backgrounds, and education to name a few.

Today's marvels of communication have not solved the problem of misunderstanding messages. Ethnic and cultural barriers still exist. Personal preferences and styles create barriers. There are regional differences. In the church, there are differences in spiritual maturity. We may react negatively to passions that come from the exercise of grace gifts (Rom. 12).

Jesus' message was difficult to grasp. The religious leaders rejected it because Jesus was a threat to their power and influence. Many people rejected it because it was difficult. He was not received because he was not what they expected. Talk about a barrier to communication; nevertheless, Jesus persisted with His message. A few caught it, and they changed the world.

Looking In: Do you stop to consider barriers to communication in your interpersonal relationships?

Looking Out: Do you (corporately) stop to evaluate the barriers to communication in your congregation? Do you make an effort to break down those barriers?

> Make it as clear as you can to all you meet that you're on their side, working with them and not against them. Help them see that the Master is about to arrive. He could show up any minute!
>
> —Philippians 4:5 (MSG)

A disciple is alert to barriers in communication.

Explain It

> And when the people of Israel heard of it, the whole assembly of the people of Israel gathered at Shiloh to make war against them.
>
> —Joshua 22:12

The actions of the eastern tribes, though innocent and God honoring, raised serious concerns among the western tribes. Honest intentions, as in this case, can lead to misunderstanding unless explained. The eastern tribes failed to communicate what they were doing and why they were doing it. What appears to be intuitively obvious to one may, because of mind-set or cultural differences, may be suspicious to others.

I recall a prayer meeting in which the leader stated that we would do things differently that evening. He set up prayer stations, lit numerous candles, and burned incense. He explained the room arrangement; he did not explain the significance of the elements in the room. It was different and appeared to be new age. I am sure it was innocent and God honoring, but I was uncomfortable.

Jesus explained His message over and over. He repeatedly stated His purpose in coming and in going. God sent the Holy Spirit at Pentecost to open the minds of the people. God is the great communicator.

Looking In: Do you take the time to consider how others may perceive your actions and intentions? Do you take the time and effort to communicate not only what you are doing but why? Do you bring others into the planning process? Or do you launch first and explain later?

Looking Out: Do you inquire of the men in your sphere of influence when they appear to be involved in questionable actions? Do you hold them accountable to clearly communicate the reasons for their actions?

> But now I am going to him who sent me, and none of you asks me, 'Where are you going?' But because I have said these things to you, sorrow has filled your heart. Nevertheless, I tell you the truth: it is to your advantage that I go away, for if I do not go away, the Helper will not come to you. But if I go, I will send him to you. And when he comes, he will convict the world concerning sin and righteousness and judgment: concerning sin, because they do not believe in me; concerning righteousness, because I go to the Father, and you will see me no longer; concerning judgment, because the ruler of this world is judged.
>
> —John 15:5–11

A disciple considers how others may perceive his actions.

Be Accountable

> … "What is this breach of faith that you have committed against the God of Israel in turning away this day from following the LORD by building yourselves an altar this day in rebellion against the LORD? Have we not had enough of the sin at Peor from which even yet we have not cleansed ourselves, and for which there came a plague upon the congregation of the LORD, that you too must turn away this day from following the LORD? **And if you too rebel against the LORD today then tomorrow he will be angry with the whole congregation of Israel.**"
>
> —Joshua 22:16–18 (emphasis added)

When Joshua released the eastern tribes, he charged them to remain faithful, be obedient, and walk in the way of the Lord. The delegation that

Eleazar the priest sent to the eastern tribes to investigate the suspicious activities was a call to accountability.

While the perceptions of the western tribes were wrong, they were holding the eastern tribes accountable. The message of the epistles is a call to accountability. Scripture is a yardstick by which we are to measure our lives. We are prone to commit "breaches of faith." We need to be held accountable. We need brothers who will challenge us in our "breaches of faith." We need brothers who will pray us through to victory in our disobediences.

A mature believer found himself caught up in a destructive behavior pattern. No matter what he tried, he could not break the pattern. He met with two brothers-in-Christ. They prayed with him that he would be liberated. The inappropriate behavior stopped.

A man was in bondage. His addiction was controlling his life. He brought several brothers-in-Christ into his confidence and they began to hold him accountable. He was liberated!

Four men in a church revealed that they were divorcing their wives. Two of the men were in a small group. The men in the group said, "No, you are not," and guided the men in restoring their marriages. The other two divorced.

Looking In: Are you in an accountability relationship? Have you agreed to be accountable to another man or group of men?

Looking Out: Do you enjoy an accountability relationship with men in your sphere of influence? Do you have an accountability agreement? Do you meet regularly to review success and failures? Do you pray for one another?

> And let us consider how to stir up one another to love and good works, not neglecting to meet together, as is the habit of some, but encouraging one another, and all the more as you see the Day drawing near.
>
> —Hebrews 10:24–25 (ESV)

A disciple is accountable.

Leave the Unclean

> **"... But now, if the land of your possession is unclean, pass over into the LORD's land where the LORD's tabernacle stands, and take for yourselves a possession among us.** Only do not rebel against the LORD or make us as rebels by building for yourselves an altar other than the altar of the LORD our God. Did not Achan the son of Zerah break faith in the matter of the devoted things, and wrath fell upon all the congregation of Israel? And he did not perish alone for his iniquity."
>
> —Joshua 22:19–20 (emphasis added)

Because the eastern tribes built the altar on the west side of the Jordan, the western tribes assumed that the land on the eastern side might be unclean. Think about the western tribes' offer: If the land is unclean or you cannot avoid the unclean among you and you are being led astray, come across the river and we will make room for you. It was a call to leave the unclean. It was a call to obedience and faithfulness.

We are in the world but not of it. We are called to engage the world. To do that, we may have to go where the Enemy is. But that does not mean we need to dwell with the Enemy. Given the western tribes' misconception, they were correct in calling the eastern tribes away from what they perceived to be willful disobedience. We need to be bold when we see men becoming trapped in lifestyles that do not honor God and undermine their testimony.

There was also an underlying but realistic fear that the perceived sin of the eastern tribes would taint the entire nation of Israel.

Looking In: In what condition is your testimony? Is it words without action? Does your life give visible evidence of your love for the Lord? Does it demonstrate obedience and joy? Are there unclean areas in your life?

Looking Out: When you become aware of a brother's disobedience, do you encourage or exhort him to leave that life? Do you encourage him to become engaged and more closely connected with believers? Do you intentionally establish a place for him to grow, like in one-on-one discipling or a small group? Do you understand the impact that his disobedience will have on the body of believers? Are you willing to confront that disobedience?

> Do all things without grumbling or questioning, that you may be blameless and innocent, children of God without blemish in the midst of a crooked and twisted generation, among whom you shine as lights in the world, holding fast to the word of life…
>
> —Philippians 2:14–16 (ESV)

A disciple encourages men to seek godly influences.

Witness

> Then Phinehas the son of Eleazar the priest, and the chiefs, returned from the people of Reuben and the people of Gad in the land of Gilead to the land of Canaan, to the people of Israel, and brought back word to them. And the report was good in the eyes of the people of Israel. And the people of Israel blessed God and spoke no more of making war against them to destroy the land where the people of Reuben and the people of Gad were settled.
> **The people of Reuben and the people of Gad called the altar Witness, "For," they said, "it is a witness between us that the LORD is God."**
>
> —Joshua 22:32–34 (emphasis added)

The eastern tribes explained that the monument near the Jordan was a witness to the Lord and the unity of a people and a nation. It was recognition of the partnership among the eastern tribes, western tribes, and the Lord. It was to be a visual reminder of the unity of a people separated by a river.

At the conclusion of this extended passage about the altar, Eleazar and Phinehas reported to Israel that the monument was acceptable. They stated that the intentions of the eastern tribes were good and honorable.

St. Francis exhorted believers to "preach the gospel and, if necessary, use words." One may argue whether words or actions are more important in advancing the gospel. In the end, however, our actions need to be consistent with our words. We are called to be "little-Christs." We are not called to build monuments; we are called to *be* monuments—monuments to a life in Christ.

A man was in a new sales job. He was not an outgoing person, yet he was selling at a rate four times the expected average. He was the lead salesman in the office for weeks running and, at one point, one of the top five salesmen on the East Coast. On several occasions in one week, customers bought what he was selling before he could give the sales pitch. He gave the Lord credit when talking to his coworkers. He is Christ to those around him—Christ-like, "a little Christ." He is a monument to life in Christ.

Looking In: What if you are the only Christ people see? How is your testimony? How is your walk?

Looking Out: Are you guiding men in your sphere of influence to a life that honors Christ? Are you in a discipling relationship that encourages a man or men in their walk?

> … for you will be a witness for him to everyone of what you have seen and heard.
>
> —Acts 22:15

A disciple's life is a witness to his faith.

Remember and Encourage

> … know for certain that the Lord your God will no longer drive out these nations before you, but they shall be a snare and a trap for you, a whip on your sides and thorns in your eyes, until you perish from off this good ground that the Lord your God has given you.
>
> —Joshua 23:13

Joshua's tenure as the leader of Israel was coming to an end. Joshua 24:29 tells us that Joshua was 110 when he died. He had served the Lord obediently and faithfully under Moses and then in leading Israel into the Promised Land. He was a model of strength, courage, and faithfulness. There is a sense of urgency in his farewell message. He reminded the people of the victories the Lord had brought them. He challenged them to complete the task the Lord had commanded. There was land yet to be conquered and people yet to be driven out with the Lord's help. Joshua warned them what would happen if they failed. He urged them to remain faithful to the Lord and not to associate with the remaining Canaanites. In case they missed what he was saying, he repeated the message.

In our highly mobile society, there will be a number of "leavings." Perhaps we will be the one leaving. Certainly there will be the leavings of others. In my military life, my family and I left nine different congregations. In the course of these tours, "hails and farewells" were a matter of routine.

Just as Joshua had a vision for the people, we must have a vision for the men we are discipling. When the time comes for us to leave, we need to reflect on what the Lord has done and encourage those who remain to stay strong in the Lord.

While there may be physical separation, e-mail and telephones allow us to continue discipling relationships. For example, several years ago we moved nine hundred miles from our previous church family. I still make weekly phone calls to one of the men in that congregation.

Looking In: When facing a "leaving," do you take time to reflect on what the Lord has done? When you must leave, do you actively reach out to men you were discipling, checking in on them from time to time to see how they are doing?

Looking Out: What might you say in a farewell message? Will you be able to recount the victories the Lord has brought you and your men? Will you be able to challenge the men to stand in the Lord in the battles that lay ahead? Will you warn your men about what will happen if the men are not faithful and obedient?

> And he said to them, "Go into all the world and proclaim the gospel to the whole creation. Whoever believes and is baptized will be saved, but whoever does not believe will be condemned.
>
> —Mark 16:15–16 (ESV)

A disciple recalls past victories and encourages others on their spiritual journeys.

Remember God's Faithfulness

> And you have seen all that the Lord your God has done to all these nations for your sake, for it is the Lord your God who has fought for you. Behold, I have allotted to you as an inheritance for your tribes those nations that remain, along with all the nations that I have already cut off, from the Jordan to the Great Sea in the west.… "… You know with all your heart and soul that not one of all the good promises the Lord your God gave you has failed. Every promise has been fulfilled; not one has failed.
>
> —Joshua 23:3–4, 14

Subduing the Promised Land was clearly an impossible task for the Israelites. They had to cross the Jordan at flood stage. Their army was no match for the Canaanites, yet fortresses were destroyed and armies defeated.

God is always asking us to do the impossible. When He asks us to do something, it is because He wants to do it. God is jealous. He wants the credit, the honor, and the glory, but He wants us to be involved. He wants us to see what He is doing. We need to see what He is doing "up close and personal." Being a disciple means doing the impossible because the Lord is in it.

A man was caught up in pornography. Just saying no, and fervent prayer, did not break the bondage. The Lord broke the bondage when the man confessed that the addiction was not glorifying God and was destroying his testimony.

A man was hesitant to step into a leadership position. With encouragement from his pastor, he began to grow as a leader. He now plays a key role in helping guide his congregation through a period of transition. He is doing the impossible because the Lord is in it.

Looking In: What is God asking you to do? Are you moving into that task with boldness and confidence? Do you believe that God is in it? Do you believe that you will be victorious in spite of appearances to the contrary?

Looking Out: What about your team? Are the team members moving forward on the basis of past victories or confidence that the Lord is committed to success in advancing the gospel? Do you keep past victories in front of your men? Is God's faithfulness a part of your refrain?

> He who calls you is faithful; he will surely do it.
>
> —1 Thessalonians 5:24

> But thanks be to God, who gives us the victory through our LORD Jesus Christ.
>
> —1 Corinthians 15:57

A disciple tackles the impossible in the power of the Lord.

Finish the Job (Again)

> Behold, I have allotted to you as an inheritance for your tribes those nations that remain, along with all the nations that I have already cut off, from the Jordan to the Great Sea in the west. **The LORD your God will push them back before you and drive them out of your sight. And you shall possess their land, just as the LORD your God promised you.**
>
> —Joshua 23:4–5 (emphasis added)

The failure of Israel to drive out the pagan inhabitants of the Promised Land is a troubling theme. Israel had rest in the land. But they permitted

Canaanites to live in their midst contrary to the Lord's command. The bottom line is that they accepted what the Lord condemned. They were complacent. They failed to finish the job.

The Canaanites represent the things in our lives that interfere with responding effectively to the Lord's call. The Lord reveals where He wants to use our time, talents, and treasure to advance His kingdom. When we do not listen and do not apply these resources as the Lord wants, we are disobedient. It is a failure of commitment or a failure to surrender completely to the Lord. These failures become Canaanites in our life.

Looking In: Have you taken inventory of the sin in your life? Have you been intentional in confessing it to the Lord and seeking repentance, or, are you satisfied to just live with it? Do you believe the Lord will remove your sin? Do you depend on the Lord to drive out your sin?

Looking Out: Are you aware of men in your sphere of influence who are struggling with sin (If we claim to be without sin, we deceive ourselves (1 John 1:10).)? Are you praying for them regularly? Are you building a relationship with one or more of them? Are you encouraging them in their walk?

> Therefore, since we are surrounded by so great a cloud of witnesses, let us also lay aside every weight, and sin which clings so closely, and let us run with endurance the race that is set before us, looking to Jesus, the founder and perfecter of our faith, who for the joy that was set before him endured the cross, despising the shame, and is seated at the right hand of the throne of God.
>
> —Hebrews 12:1–2 (ESV)

A disciple is persistent in removing sin from his life.

Be Very Strong and Obey the Lord

> Therefore, be very strong to keep and to do all that is written in the Book of the Law of Moses, turning aside from it neither to the right hand nor to the left …
>
> —Joshua 23:6

Joshua's farewell message is not about Joshua. It is about the Lord and what He did for Israel. It is about the need to remain faithful. What the Lord did, He did through Joshua. Joshua was faithful, strong, and courageous. Joshua commanded the Israelites to be strong in their obedience.

The Lord commands us to be strong and courageous and tells us that He will be with us. We are to be obedient to the Word. He commands us to turn to neither the right nor the left. We are not to muddle through. We are to be victorious. We are more than conquerors! Obedience is the key to victory.

Obedience is serious business. It is hard work. It takes strength to stay on the obedience path. We need to be intentional in avoiding turns to the right or the left. Joshua challenged Israel to continue the process of possessing the land and not mix with the occupants. Strength is needed to be obedient and accomplish what the Lord has commanded. There is no other way to enjoy the blessings of the Lord.

A question was raised in a Sunday school class: do you consider yourself a strong person? The answer is "no." Our strength comes from the Lord; obedience is from the Lord.

Looking In: Are you steadfast and intentional in obedience? Are *strength*, *faithfulness*, and *courage* words that describe your life? Are you aware of the Holy Spirit helping you avoid sin and overcome hidden faults? When you sin, do you grieve over your disobedience? Do you earnestly seek a new direction in obedience? Do you believe that the Lord is with you and will give you victory in your battles?

Looking Out: Are the men in your sphere of influence obedient? Do you have an accountability relationship with a few of them? Are you encouraging your men in their spiritual walk? Finally, are you transparent in front of your men as you deal with disobedience? Do you model obedience?

> Finally, be strong in the Lord and in the strength of his might.
>
> —Ephesians 6:10

> ... By this we know that we love the children of God, when we love God and obey his commandments.
>
> —1 John 5:2

A disciple is strong and obedient.

Love the Lord

> ... that you may not mix with these nations remaining among you or make mention of the names of their gods or swear by them or serve them or bow down to them, but you shall cling to the Lord your God just as you have done to this day.... **Be very careful, therefore, to love the Lord your God.** For if you turn back and cling to the remnant of these nations remaining among you and make marriages with them, so that you associate with them and they with you, know for certain that the Lord your God will no longer drive out these nations before you, but they shall be a snare and a trap for you, a whip on your sides and thorns in your eyes, until you perish from off this good ground that the Lord your God has given you.
>
> —Joshua 23:7–13 (emphasis added)

Joshua warned Israel not to be taken in by the pagan culture of the Canaanites. He repeats the warning the Lord gave him earlier (Joshua in 1:7-8). He was concerned about the Canaanites' poisoning influence on Israel.

We are called to be in the world but not of the world. We are a holy people. We are to be separate from the culture of the world. The gods of this world beckon us to bow to power, possessions, and position. When we are driven by these goals, they come between us and the Lord, we break our connection with Him, and we no longer seek to follow His will.

A man succumbed on many occasions to acquiring worldly things. He put wants ahead of needs and his income would not support his family. His poor judgment in attempting to recover only drove him deeper in debt. Finally his wife divorced him and took the children.

Looking In: Are you aware of the influence of the world in your life? Think about your possessions. Do they glorify God? Is your life different from the world around you? Are you in an accountability relationship with other men? Is the Lord the love of your life?

Looking Out: Are any of your men consumed or distracted by the things of the world? Are they influenced by the worldly culture? Have you built a trusting relationship with other men? Are you in an accountability relationship with them?

> Jesus replied, "'Love the LORD your God with all your heart and with all your soul and with all your mind.' This is the first and greatest commandment. And the second is like it: 'Love your neighbor as yourself.'"
>
> —Matthew 22:37

A disciple loves the Lord and not the things of this world.

Encourage and Warn

> "… if you transgress the covenant of the LORD your God, which he commanded you, and go and serve other gods and bow down to them. Then the anger of the LORD will be kindled against you, and you shall perish quickly from off the good land that he has given to you."
>
> —Joshua 23:16

As Joshua prepared to hand off the reins of leadership, he encouraged the people of Israel to remain true to the Lord and warned them of the consequences if they did not. The Lord does not keep the consequences of disobedience a secret. Joshua reminded Israel, and his words are a reminder to us. With obedience comes blessing (Deut. 26:1–14), and with disobedience comes curses (Deut. 28:15–68).

Do we take the warnings from the Lord seriously? Not only does the Lord warn us about disobedience, He empowers us, through the Holy Spirit, to overcome sin.

Looking In: What are the areas of disobedience in your life? Are you dealing with them? Are you under conviction? Are you bringing the issue or issues under the power of the Holy Spirit? Is the Lord revealing your hidden faults? Do you believe that, with the power of God, you can overcome sin? Are you claiming victory?

Looking Out: Are you encouraging the men around you to be obedient? Do you have an open and honest relationship with at least one other man in which you hold each other accountable? Are you encouraging them to identify disobedience?

> And we urge you, brothers, warn those who are idle, encourage the timid, help the weak, be patient with everyone.
>
> —1 Thessalonians 5:14

A disciple encourages and warns his brothers.

Prepare Those Who Follow

> "And now I am about to go the way of all the earth, and you know in your hearts and souls, all of you, that not one word has failed of all the good things that the Lord your God promised concerning you. All have come to pass for you; not one of them has failed. But just as all the good things that the Lord your God promised concerning you

> have been fulfilled for you, so the LORD will bring upon you all the evil things, until he has destroyed you from off this good land that the LORD your God has given you, if you transgress the covenant of the LORD your God, which he commanded you, and go and serve other gods and bow down to them. Then the anger of the LORD will be kindled against you, and you shall perish quickly from off the good land that he has given to you."
>
> —Joshua 23:14–16 (emphasis added)

Joshua understood that his time of leadership was coming to a close. During his tenure the land had been conquered and divided among the tribes. The leadership moved from a single person to the elders of the tribes (Judg. 2:7). The elders had been with Joshua. They had seen the Lord work on their behalf. They had been discipled.

This is the second transition in leadership in the book of Joshua. Moses mentored Joshua for forty years. Joshua mentored the elders of Israel for at least twenty-five years. He prepared them for leadership. Mentoring is the process of connecting with less mature believers for the purpose of developing spiritual maturity and ministry skills. There will always be transitions in leadership. We need to be preparing others to pick up the mantle of leadership or responsibility when we leave the scene. We are called to prepare others to follow us.

Mentoring requires a relationship of mutual trust and respect. It takes more than just shaking hands in the foyer on Sunday morning. It happens over coffee, or a meal, or on the playing field, or during workdays. Note that Jesus spent the first half of His ministry building relationships with His disciples. In the second half, He focused on teaching the disciples.

Looking In: Who is discipling you? Who is your mentor? How much time does he spend with you? What are you learning from him?

Looking Out: Who are you discipling? Who are you preparing to step into leadership? Do these men see the victories in your life? Are they experiencing victories in their own lives? Do they demonstrate leadership qualities?

> I'm passing this work on to you, my son Timothy. The prophetic word that was directed to you prepared us for this. All those prayers are coming together now so you will do this well, fearless in your struggle, keeping a firm grip on your faith and on yourself. After all, this is a fight we're in.
>
> —1 Timothy 1:18–19 (MSG)

A disciple prepares those who will follow.

Remember the Covenant

Remember and Renew (HIStory)

> Then Joshua assembled all the tribes of Israel at Shechem. He summoned the elders, leaders, judges and officials of Israel, and they presented themselves before God.
>
> Joshua said to all the people, "**This is what the LORD, the God of Israel, says:** 'Long ago your forefathers, including Terah the father of Abraham … and Nahor, lived beyond the River and worshiped other gods. But I took your father Abraham …
>
> "'…When I brought your fathers out of Egypt, you came to the sea, … Then you lived in the desert for a long time.
>
> "'I brought you to the land of the Amorites who lived east of the Jordan. … When Balak son of Zippor, the king of Moab, prepared to fight against Israel, …
>
> "'Then you crossed the Jordan and came to Jericho. … So I gave you a land on which you did not toil and cities you did not build; and you live in them and eat from vineyards and olive groves that you did not plant.'"
>
> —Joshua 24:1–13 (emphasis added)

"Thus says the Lord …" The Lord recounts the history of Israel from the time of Terah to the conquest of the Promised Land. History is important to the Lord because it is about what He has done. He wants us to focus on what He has done. Joshua's message was to all Israel, with specific attention to the leadership. The leadership needs to know the Lord and remember His actions. They need to see the past as what the Lord has done.

As we disciple men, it is important to look at what the Lord has done and is doing. It is His story, not ours. By reflecting on what God has done in the past, we strengthen our faith in what He will do today, tomorrow, and in the future. The Lord wants us to meditate on what He has done. We see God most clearly in the rear view mirror, not through the windshield.

Looking In: What is your perspective on the past? Do your thoughts turn to what you have done, or to what the Lord has done? Who is at the center of your testimony? Is your testimony about you, or is it about the Lord? What is your life's focus? What did the Lord do in your life this year, this month, this week, and/or today?

Looking Out: Do you help your men see the relationship between God's actions in the past, in the current age, and in His plan for the future? Like Joshua, do you take time to review what the Lord has done and is doing?

> But I also want you to think about how this keeps your significance from getting blown up into self-importance. For no matter how significant you are, it is only because of what you are a part of.
>
> —1 Corinthians 12:19 (MSG)

A disciple is aware of what God has done and is doing in his life.

Choose Whom You Will Serve

Decide

> "Now therefore fear the LORD and serve him in sincerity and in faithfulness. Put away the gods that your fathers served beyond the River and in Egypt, and serve the LORD. And if it is evil in your eyes to serve the LORD, choose this day whom you will serve, whether the gods your fathers served in the region beyond the River, or the gods of the Amorites in whose land you dwell. **But as for me and my house, we will serve the LORD."**
>
> —Joshua 24:14–15 (emphasis added)

Joshua exhorted the people to serve the Lord. He urged them to set the example. He followed up by his own commitment to follow the Lord. He and his family would serve the Lord. They would not serve the gods of their ancestors (in Mesopotamia and Egypt) or the gods of the Canaanites. Whether we admit it or not, this is a challenge. We are confronted daily with the gods of our culture and perhaps even the gods of the culture of our ancestors. Salvation is a choice. Discipleship is a choice.

A men's leader began to pray diligently for a friend with significant issues in his life. He was not strongly connected to his church. Things began to change in the man's life and he became more involved in church and the men's small group. About nine months after joining the group he died of cancer. There was a major change in the group's discussions. The man's death caused the men to focus more seriously on their lives and how seriously they took their relationship with the Lord.

Looking In: Do you recognize the gods that confront you daily? What do you serve: power, prestige, possessions, position? Do you choose each day to serve the Lord?

Looking Out: Do you model that choice in front of your families, friends, neighbors, and community?

> … set the believers an example in speech, in conduct, in love, in faith, in purity.
>
> —1 Timothy 4:12

A disciple makes the choice to serve the Lord daily.

Serve the Lord

> Then the people answered, "Far be it from us that we should forsake the LORD to serve other gods, for it is the LORD our God who brought us and our fathers up from the land of Egypt, out of the house of slavery, and who did those great signs in our sight and preserved us in all the way that we went, and among all the peoples through whom we passed.… **Therefore we also will serve the LORD, for he is our God."** But Joshua said to the people, **"You are not able to serve the LORD, for he is a holy God**. He is a jealous God; he will not forgive your transgressions or your sins. If you forsake the LORD and serve foreign gods, then he will turn and do you harm and consume you, after having done you good." And the people said to Joshua, "No, but we will serve the LORD." Then Joshua said to the people, "You are witnesses against yourselves that you have chosen the LORD to serve him." **And they said, "We are witnesses." He said, "Then put away the foreign gods that are among you, and incline your heart to the LORD, the God of Israel." And the**

> **people said to Joshua, "The Lord our God we will serve, and his voice we will obey."**
>
> —Joshua 23:16–24 (emphasis added)

Joshua challenged the Israelites to choose whom they would serve. They responded with a commitment to serve the Lord. Joshua, however, perceived that they were committing to serve out of their own strength. He urged them to put action to their words, "Then put away the foreign gods that are among you …" He further instructed them to "incline your heart to the Lord." Their commitment needed to be from the heart, not the mind. They responded again that they would serve the Lord. Then He asked why there were still foreign gods in their midst. They needed to put action to their words.

It is impossible for us to serve the Lord. Only in the power of the Lord can we be resolute in our service. Only through the power of the Holy Spirit can we succeed in doing His will. Being obedient takes more than determination.

Looking In: Are you depending on the Lord for faithfulness and obedience? What are the distractions in your life? Are you eliminating the "foreign gods?" Are you relying on your own strength and will power to overcome distractions, or are you calling on the Lord?

Looking Out: Do you challenge your men to submit to the Lord? Are you challenging them to make Christ the Lord of their lives? Who among your men are serving "foreign gods"? Are they aware of distractions and the consequences of becoming trapped by them? Are you coming alongside these men and encouraging them in their walk with the Lord?

> And this I say for your own profit, not that I may put a leash on you, but for what is proper, and that you may serve the Lord without distraction.
>
> —1 Corinthians 7:35 (NKJV)

A disciple eliminates distractions.

Be a Witness

> So Joshua made a covenant with the people that day, and put in place statutes and rules for them at Shechem. And Joshua wrote these words in the Book of the Law of God. And he took a large stone and set it up there under the terebinth that was by the sanctuary of the LORD. And Joshua said to all the people, "Behold, this stone shall be a witness against us, for it has heard all the words of the LORD that he spoke to us. **Therefore it shall be a witness against you, lest you deal falsely with your God."** So Joshua sent the people away, every man to his inheritance.
>
> —Joshua 24:25–28 (emphasis added)

This is the seventh monument mentioned in the book of Joshua. This monument was a reminder to Israel to serve the Lord. It was to be a permanent reminder of the Lord's command of obedience.

1. The crossing of the Jordan
2. Achan's grave
3. The victory at Ai
4. The reminder of the law
5. The victory at Gibeon
6. The unity of the tribes
7. The stone of witness

Each generation needs to set memorials to what the Lord has done. There need to be markers that remind us of God's faithfulness. Reminders of failures and victories are important. Scripture is a critical reminder of our shortcomings and the power of the Lord to bring victory. The Word of God is not effective unless we personalize it. Then as we read, we need to mark the victories over our shortcomings.

Looking In: Is there a strategically placed marker in your life that reminds you to be obedient? Do you have a Scripture verse on the bathroom mirror? Do you have an open Bible on your desk or near your computer? What is the message of these markers? Is it "I must be obedient." Or is it, "Lord, help me to be obedient?"

Looking Out: Are you assisting men in your sphere of influence to set markers in their lives? Are you helping them understand the difference between obedience in their own strength and will power or an obedience empowered by the Holy Spirit?

> The whole assembly became silent as they listened to Barnabas and Paul telling about the miraculous signs and wonders God had done among the Gentiles through them.
>
> —Acts 15:12

A disciple posts reminders that obedience comes through surrender.

Recognize the Seasons of Life

Leave a Legacy

> After these things Joshua the son of Nun, the servant of the Lord, died, being 110 years old. And they buried him in his own inheritance at Timnath-serah, which is in the hill country of Ephraim, north of the mountain of Gaash. **Israel served the Lord all the days of Joshua, and all the days of the elders who outlived Joshua and had known all the work that the Lord did for Israel**.
>
> —Joshua 24:29–31 (emphasis added)

Joshua remained faithful to the end. The elders remained faithful to the end. They saw and remembered all that the Lord had done. These words are disturbing. They imply that Israel did not follow the Lord after the elders passed from the scene. Of course, that is true. Thereafter came cycles of disobedience and obedience. In spite of warnings from the Lord, the Israelites succumbed to the pagan influences of the Canaanites. They failed to heed Joshua's admonitions and warnings. They did not remove the foreign gods in spite of their covenant to serve the Lord. Israel forgot their covenant with the Lord.

Verse 31 is a transition bridging the spiritual divide between the obedience of Israel in the book of Joshua and the disobedience of Israel described in the book of Judges.

Is there a temptation to say, "How could they do that?" Look at your life this day. Have you fallen for something that is important in our culture but not to the Lord?

This is about more than staying the course. It is about a transition in leadership. It is about leaving a legacy. It appears that the elders did not keep the faithfulness of the Lord front and center. They were not persistent in eliminating the Canaanites. They did not set an example.

Looking In: Have you forgotten what the Lord has done in your life? Do you keep a journal? Do you keep your testimony fresh and current?

Looking Out: Do you build up the body? Do you encourage those around you with reports on what the Lord is doing? What will your legacy be? What are you leaving for the next generation? Will there be faithful men who follow you, who will continually remind the people of what God has done?

> You then, my child, be strengthened by the grace that is in Christ Jesus, and what you have heard from me in the presence of many witnesses entrust to faithful men who will be able to teach others also.
>
> —2 Timothy 2:1–2 (ESV)

A disciple keeps it going.

Have Faith

> As for the bones of Joseph, which the people of Israel brought up from Egypt, they buried them at Shechem, in the piece of land that Jacob bought from the sons of Hamor the father of Shechem for a hundred pieces of money. It became an inheritance of the descendants of Joseph.
>
> —Joshua 24:32

Joseph's remains were buried on land bought by his father, Jacob. This is about the legacy of the patriarchs. There is no rest for those outside of the Promised Land. Joseph's bones had been kept for more than four hundred years. Now that Israel occupied the Promised Land, Joseph's remains could join those of Abraham, Isaac, and Jacob. The Israelites kept his remains until the time they would return to the land of the patriarchs. Israel was now a nation. It enjoyed a blessed relationship with God. Years of slavery and wandering were over. The Lord had given the people rest. Joseph could be buried.

The bones of Joseph are a reminder of God's faithfulness. The Lord kept His promise to the children of Israel (Gen. 48:1–4). He brought them out of Egypt and gave them the Promised Land. The bones of Joseph are also a reminder of Joseph's faith. He believed that God would rescue Israel and provide rest in the Promised Land (Gen. 50:22–26).

Today, the bones of Joseph are a reminder of God's promise to rescue us in the last days. God kept His promise to Joseph and He will keep His promise to us. Like Joseph, we need to keep the faith. We need to believe that God will remove the church in the last days (the rapture) as He promised.

Looking In: Are you through wandering? Have you received spiritual renewal and restoration? Are you in the "land" the Lord has given you? Is the Lord giving you rest? Do you believe in the Rapture?

Looking Out: Do you know men who have yet to receive eternal life and the abundant life? Are you helping them to make that journey? Do you remind your men that God will remove His church in the last days?

> Therefore, since the promise of entering his rest still stands, let us be careful that none of you be found to have fallen short of it. For we also have had the gospel preached to us, just as they did; but the message they heard was of no value to them, because those who heard did not combine it with faith. Now we who have believed enter that rest, just as God has said.
>
> —Hebrews 4:1–3

A disciple trusts the Lord.

Move On

> And Eleazar the son of Aaron died, and they buried him at Gibeah, the town of Phinehas his son, which had been given him in the hill country of Ephraim.
>
> —Joshua 23:33

Joshua was dead. Joseph's bones were buried. With Eleazar's death, an age in Israel's history came to an end. The leadership of Israel was dead and buried. It was time to move on. It was time to complete the task. However, no strong spiritual leader followed. Again and again Israel failed to keep the covenant with the Lord.

When we experience the loss of a spiritual leader in our lives, it is essential to seek a new one. When we lose an accountability partner or partners, we need to establish new ones. True, the Lord is the ultimate spiritual leader. However, Scripture is replete with examples of human spiritual leaders (priests, elders, disciples). The history of Israel shows the consequences when there are no godly leaders.

Looking In: Who is your spiritual leader? Is he a man of strong Christian character? Does he exhibit the qualifications of an elder? Is he a man of vision? Is he a disciplemaker? Are you in an accountability relationship?

Looking Out: Are you a spiritual leader to those around you? Are you leading men to the throne of grace and encouraging them to walk with the Lord? Are you intentional in these connections?

> Not that I have already obtained this or am already perfect, but I press on to make it my own, because Christ Jesus has made me his own. Brothers, I do not consider that I have made it my own. But one thing I do: forgetting what lies behind and straining forward to what lies ahead, I press on toward the goal for the prize of the upward call of God in Christ Jesus.
>
> —Philippians 3:12–14

A disciple makes disciples who make disciples.

Trust and Obey

Encounter the Lord and Submit to Him

The Lord Is Present. Therefore, Be Connected.

> After the death of Moses the servant of the LORD, **the LORD said to Joshua** son of Nun, … "Have I not commanded you? Be strong and courageous. Do not be terrified; do not be discouraged, **for the LORD your God will be with you wherever you go."**
>
> —Joshua 1:1, 9 (emphasis added)

On thirteen occasions, the Lord spoke to Joshua. On other occasions Joshua engaged the Lord. Clearly, Joshua was tuned to God's frequency. Joshua's greatest quality was his personal connection with the Lord. God called him to lead Israel into the Promised Land. He listened for the Lord. He listened to the Lord. He was connected to the Lord.

There is a difference between the Lord's presence and His involvement. The Lord is always present. He is *always* there (*Jehovah Shammah*). He promised to be with us as long as we are obedient. When we disobey, we separate ourselves from Him. However, we can be encouraged by the fact that He is always there and will welcome us back.

As disciples, it is imperative that we be connected to the Lord. The Lord speaks to us in different ways. He speaks through His Word; He personalizes the Word. He plants thoughts and ideas in our mind. He speaks through open or closed doors. He speaks through others.

Looking In: Do you expect God to speak to you? Do you listen to Him during your prayer time? What is He saying to you through His Word? What is He saying in your walk with Him? Are you enjoying the presence of the Lord? Can you tell when you have moved outside of His presence? Do you know how to get back into His presence?

Looking Out: Do you ask the men in your sphere of influence what God is doing in their lives? Do you ask them what God is saying in His Word? Are you encouraging your men to listen for God; to listen to God? Do you create expectations that God speaks personally?

> Then Jesus said, "He who has ears to hear, let him hear."
>
> —Mark 4:9

> God did this so that men would seek him and perhaps reach out for him and find him, though he is not far from each one of us.
>
> —Acts 17:27

A disciple stays connected to the Lord.

The Lord Is All Powerful. Therefore, Be Bold.

> … the water from upstream stopped flowing. **It piled up in a heap a great distance away …**
>
> —Joshua 3:16 (emphasis added)

> … the people shouted a great shout, and **the wall fell down flat.**
>
> —Joshua 6:20 (ESV) (emphasis added)

> **The sun stopped in the middle of the sky** and delayed going down about a full day.
>
> —Joshua 10:13 (emphasis added)

The Lord demonstrated incredible power in leading Israel across the Jordan at flood stage. He demonstrated incredible power when He collapsed the walls of Jericho inward. He demonstrated incredible power in giving Israel victory after victory. He had command over the elements and over Canaanite armies. Nothing stood in His way.

We see God as too small. We see the challenges we face through human eyes. Our vision is limited by human weakness, human wisdom, and human weariness. The Lord wants us to see things in terms of His wisdom, vision, and power. To do that, we need to transfer control to Him.

The Lord wants to do great things in our lives. He wants to do great things in the lives of others through us. He gives us God-sized tasks and empowers us to carry them out. Ben Stine said, "Faith is not believing that God can; it is knowing that God will."

A man was hired by a retail company with the agreement that he would not have to work on Sundays. One day his boss scheduled him to work on Sunday and asked him if he could make an exception this one time because his services were needed. He told her he would pray about it. That evening he asked his men's group to pray about it. The next day he discovered that he was not scheduled to work on Sunday. He thanked his manager who told him that the store was over payroll and she had to cut back on hours. The man was bold in setting the conditions for his employment. He was bold in bringing the matter to the Lord.

Looking In: Is Joshua's Lord your Lord? Do you know that the Lord's power is available to you? He has called you to a God-sized task. Are you experiencing His power behind you?

Looking Out: Are the men around you tapping into the power available to them? Are they moving out boldly in faith? Are you encouraging boldness? Are you modeling boldness?

> Jumping out of the boat, Peter walked on the water to Jesus.
>
> —Matthew 14:28–29 (ESV)

> Jesus looked at them and said, "With man this is impossible, but not with God; all things are possible with God."
>
> —Mark 10:27

> And with great power the apostles were giving their testimony to the resurrection of the LORD Jesus, and great grace was upon them all.
>
> —Acts 4:33 (ESV)

A disciple boldly steps out in faith.

The Lord Is Persistent. Therefore, Stay the Course.

> Then the LORD said to Joshua … For I have delivered into your hands the king of Ai, his people, his city and his land.
>
> —Joshua 8:1

The Lord's persistence is demonstrated at Ai. Israel had failed in the first battle, but the Lord got Joshua's attention and gave directions for a second attack. The Lord promised Israel a return to the land of the patriarchs. He was not about to let the failure at Ai stop progress.

Scripture is replete with other examples of the Lord's persistence. The Lord called Samuel until he responded. The Lord appointed Saul king. Saul made a detour. The Lord offered him opportunities to get with the program. Saul failed and the Lord set David in his place. The Lord persisted. The children of Israel turned to pagan gods, and the Lord sent Israel into exile in Babylon. But the Lord rescued a remnant and restored them to Jerusalem. The Lord persisted. God's plan was for His people to be witnesses to the nations. Israel failed. He sent Jesus to save the world. Today the message of salvation is spreading around the world. The Lord is persisting.

Jesus was persistent. He set His eyes on the cross and never wavered. Mark, in his gospel (ESV), uses the word "immediately" thirty-six times to describe Jesus' actions. Bob Wenz, in his book, *Navigating Your Perfect Storm*, uses the word "resolute" to describe Jesus' persistence in moving to the cross. The Lord is resolute in reaching out to us. He made the supreme effort. Are you resolute in staying the course?

Looking In: What is your calling? What is your gifting? Where are you using your spiritual gifts? Are you faithful to your calling? Are you resolute in pursuing your calling?

Looking Out: Are you making disciples? Are you resolute in leading a man or men to the throne of grace and into the spirit-filled life? Are you helping your men discover their grace gift? Are you encouraging them to be faithful to their calling?

> I was most happy when some friends arrived and brought the news that you persist in following the way of Truth. Nothing could make me happier than getting reports that my children continue diligently in the way of Truth!
>
> —3 John 1:3–4 (MSG)

> Be faithful, even to the point of death, and I will give you the crown of life.
>
> —Revelation 2:10

A disciple resolves to stay the course.

The Lord Is All Knowing. Therefore, Stop and Ask Directions.

> The LORD said to Joshua, …
>
> —Joshua 2:7

> "When you see the ark of the covenant of the LORD your God, and the priests, who are Levites, carrying it, you are to move out from your positions and follow it. **Then you will know which way to go, since you have never been this way before."**
>
> —Joshua 3:3–4 (emphasis added)

> So the men took some of their provisions, **but did not ask counsel from the LORD.**
>
> —Joshua 9:14 (emphasis added)

There is constant dialogue between Joshua and the Lord. Joshua sought the Lord for direction. There were times when the Lord challenged Joshua. When Joshua sought the Lord's direction or listened to Him, Israel was victorious. When the people presumed to know the way, Israel was defeated (Ai – chapter 7) or accepting (Gibeon – chapter 9). The conquest of the Promised Land was remarkable. God was the chief architect of the victories. He was the supreme strategist. He was the ultimate tactician. He knew how to do it.

The Lord told Joshua to place the ark of the covenant in front of the army "… since you have not been this way before." He is saying to Israel and to us, "I want to be in front of everything you do!"

Success breeds contentment. We find ourselves saying things like, "This is easy," "It is a no-brainer," or "I've got the answer." The message in Joshua is that no matter how simple things appear, seek the Lord's guidance. Scripture is clear: seldom did the Lord do things the same way twice.

God wants to be the chief architect of our lives and of our victories. He wants to be the supreme strategist. He wants to be our ultimate tactician.

Looking In: How constant is your dialogue with the Lord? Are you tempted to do things on your own? Do you pray first? Do you stop to listen? Do you seek the counsel of others? Are you doing things your way or God's way? Do you ask for guidance only on the big decisions? Do you rely on the One who knows the way? Are you modeling what it means to inquire of the Lord?

Looking Out: Are you aware of men who are muddling through life? Are you in relationships in which men are open about the direction of their lives and the decisions they are making? Are you encouraging them to listen to the Lord?

> If any of you lacks wisdom, let him ask God, who gives generously to all without reproach, and it will be given him. But let him ask in faith, with no doubting …
>
> —James 1:5–6

A disciple asks for direction from the Lord.

The Lord Provides. Therefore, Ask Him.

> Now then, you and all these people, get ready to cross the Jordan River into the land I am about to give to them—to the Israelites. **I will give you every place where you set your foot**, as I promised Moses.
>
> —Joshua 1:2–3 (emphasis added)

> The day after the Passover**, that very day, they ate some of the produce of the land: unleavened bread and roasted grain**. The manna stopped the day after they ate this food from the land; there was no longer any manna for the Israelites, but that year they ate of the produce of Canaan.
>
> —Joshua 5:11–12 (emphasis added)

The Lord gave Israel the Promised Land. He made it possible for them to enter and possess the land. He provided the land and its abundant resources.

The Lord gave manna to Israel from the crossing of the Red Sea until the Passover at Gilgal. He provided manna five days a week and a double portion on the sixth for the Sabbath. He did this for 40 years. They did not have to work for it. All they had to do was gather it. The Lord made the produce of the Promised Land available to Israel; He provided food. They did not work for it. All they had to do was gather it. He provided variety.

In the fall of 2010, Child Evangelism Fellowship in southern Sudan held a children's camp. When there were a number of problems getting the children to the camp, a man agreed to provide free transportation. The staff had only enough food for 120 children. One-hundred-fifty children showed up. The staff prayed, reminding Jesus that He had fed five thousand with five loaves and two fish. As a result, everyone had enough to eat and there was food left over!

Looking In: Are you counting the blessings of the Lord? Is the life you enjoy the result of the work of your hands, or is it from the Lord?

Looking Out: Are you helping the men around you count their blessings? Are you encouraging your men to recognize and understand what the Lord has provided?

> And he directed the people to sit down on the grass. Taking the five loaves and the two fish and looking up to heaven, he gave thanks and broke the loaves. Then he gave them to the disciples, and the disciples gave them to the people … They all ate and were satisfied, and the disciples picked up twelve basketfuls of broken pieces that were left over. The number of those who ate was about five thousand men, besides women and children.
>
> —Matthew 14:9–21

A disciple knows that the Lord will provide.

The Lord Demands Allegiance. Therefore, Be Vigilant.

> Be very careful, **therefore, to love the Lord your God**.
>
> —Joshua 23:11 (emphasis added)

> But as for me and my house, we will serve the Lord.
>
> —Joshua 24:15

Joshua warned the people about disobedience. Israel was supposed to drive out the Canaanites to avoid falling into pagan practices. Israel was commanded to remove anything that would tempt them into disobedience. Israel was to remain faithful. Joshua made it a family matter. He drew a line in the sand. He exhorted the people and followed that by a personal commitment.

The Lord is very clear. Do not have other gods before Him, make no graven images, do not take the Lord's name in vain, and keep the Sabbath holy (Ex. 20:3–8). However, Israel failed to obey these commandments. They began worshiping Canaanite gods and took Canaanite wives. As a result, the Lord permitted Israel to suffer at the hands of her enemies.

Jesus brought the first four commandments under the new covenant when He said, "Love the Lord your God with all your heart, with all your soul and with all your mind" (Matt. 22:37). The temptations of our pagan culture surround us. The things in our environment are magnets that pull us away from our devotion and submission to God. God makes it clear: if we are vigilant in staying clear of the unholy, He will bless us. If we fail, we will suffer the consequences of disobedience. We are called to be vigilant. The message is clear: God's blessings come through obedience.

Looking In: What are the distractions in your life? Do you stop periodically and take inventory? Have you cleaned house recently? Are you faithful to the Lord? Do you seek comfort and "blessings" from the things of the world?

Looking Out: What are the things in the lives of your men that distract from their love of the Lord? Do you spend time with your men reviewing distractions? Are you praying together against the inroads of our culture?

> … Therefore go out from their midst, and be separate from them, says the Lord, and touch no unclean thing; then I will welcome you, and I will be a father to you, and you shall be sons and daughters to me, says the Lord Almighty.
>
> —1 Corinthians 6:17–18

A disciple is vigilant in avoiding things that distract from the Lord.

The Lord Demands Obedience. Therefore, Keep His Commands.

> **Be careful to obey all the law my servant Moses gave you; do not turn from it to the right or to the left, that you may be successful wherever you go.** Do not let this Book of the Law depart from your mouth; meditate on it day and night, so that you may be careful to do everything written in it. Then you will be prosperous and successful.
>
> —Joshua 1:7–8 (emphasis added)

> Be very strong; **be careful to obey all that is written in the Book of the Law of Moses, without turning aside to the right or to the left** ...
>
> —Joshua 23:6 (emphasis added)

The Lord admonished Israel to obey the Laws He had given them. He repeated this admonition three times in Joshua. He told them of the benefits of obedience. He told them of the consequences if they did not obey. The history of Israel is a cycle of obedience and disobedience. It is a cycle of blessings and curses.

God promised to be with Israel and then demonstrated it on a day-to-day basis. A major lesson from the book of Joshua is that God's guidance depends on our obedience. Dietrich Bonhoeffer said that faith follows obedience. We experience God's involvement in our lives when we are obedient.

Jesus called His disciples to obedience. He summarized commandments 5 through 10 with these words, "Love your neighbor as yourself" (Matt. 22:39). These commandments are essential in our relationships with others. God has given us the Holy Spirit to enable us to be obedient.

Looking In: On a scale of one to ten, what is your level of obedience? Is obedience something you are trying to do on your own? Or are you depending on the Holy Spirit to keep you in obedience? Do you stop and take inventory of obedience and disobedience in your life? When you fail, do you just try harder? Or do you bring it to the Lord, the keeper of the covenant?

Looking Out: Do your men understand the relationship between obedience and blessings? Do you discuss this with your men?

> And this is love: that we walk in obedience to his commands. As you have heard from the beginning, his command is that you walk in love.
>
> —2 John 1:6

A disciple lives out the love of Christ Jesus.

The Lord Is Faithful. Therefore, Believe.

> Not one word of all the good promises that the LORD had made to the house of Israel had failed; all came to pass.
>
> —Joshua 21:45

God had a plan for Israel. He revealed His plan and then He carried it out. He made it happen. Israel's success was not due to a well-trained and equipped army; it was due to a God-given strategy and His personal intervention.

We are under the new covenant. The Lord promised from the time of the fall that He would send the Messiah. He was faithful to that promise. Therefore, as believers, we live under the righteousness of Christ. Not only that, He promised to give us, as His disciples, the Holy Spirit to guard and guide us. As disciples, we have the Holy Spirit. As He left this earthly life He promised, "I am with you always, to the end of the age" (Matt. 28:20).

God is here! God has a plan to advance His kingdom. He is always at work carrying out His plan. He is faithful in our individual lives. He is faithful in meeting the needs of His church.

What more can the Lord say to us? What more can He do for us? He is faithful. In turn, He calls us to be faithful. If we do not experience challenges in carrying out His plan, we may not be on His path. We are called to believe that He will do it. He will do it.

Looking In: How has the Lord been faithful to you? Where are you seeing the Lord work? What are you doing to advance His kingdom? Are you carrying out His calling, trusting that He will help you live it out? Do you routinely stop to consider how He has kept His promises?

Looking Out: Do your men recognize God's faithfulness? Do you ask your men what the Lord is doing in their lives? Do they give testimonies about God's faithfulness? Is there an expectation among your men that God is acting on their behalf?

> What if some did not have faith? Will their lack of faith nullify God's faithfulness? Not at all!
>
> —Romans 3:3–4

> For everyone who has been born of God overcomes the world. And this is the victory that has overcome the world—our faith. Who is it that overcomes the world except the one who believes that Jesus is the Son of God?
>
> —1 John 5:4–5

A disciple advances on the basis of faith.

The Lord Is All Knowing. Therefore, Make Wise Choices.

> "... choose this day whom you will serve."
>
> —Joshua 24:15

The book of Joshua is filled with people making choices. Rahab chose to follow the Lord; Jericho chose to hunker down. Achan chose to take things devoted to the Lord; Israel chose to make a covenant with the Gibeonites. Five kings chose to attack the Gibeonites; Israel chose to go to the aid of the Gibeonites. And so it went.

Not only do we need to ask the Lord for direction, we need to make wise choices. On two occasions Joshua did not ask for directions, and Israel encountered problems.

Making wise choices depends on one's connection with the Lord. Wise choices depend on seeking direction through His word and prayer. Otherwise, one depends on one's own wisdom and strength for survival.

Wise choices come from giving the Lord control of our lives. The Lord gives us choices. He expects us to respond to His offering of eternal life, peace, and rest. Joshua exhorted the people to "choose this day …" Making wise choices is a daily, moment-by-moment choice.

Looking In: Did you choose to give the Lord control today? What choices lay in front of you today? Have you brought them to the Lord?

Looking Out: Do you take time with your men to review the choices available to them and their benefits or consequences? Do your men understand the fundamental choices of salvation and lordship?

> I speak in human terms because of the weakness of your flesh. For just as you presented your members as slaves of uncleanness, and of lawlessness leading to more lawlessness, so now present your members as slaves of righteousness for holiness.
>
> —Romans 6:19 (NKJV)

A disciple seeks the Lord's counsel in making choices.

The Lord Is Always Advancing. Therefore, Advance Together.

> The people of Reuben and the people of Gad called the altar Witness, "For," they said, **"it is a witness between us that the Lord is God."**
>
> —Joshua 22:34 (emphasis added)

The book of Joshua is about a spiritual journey, our spiritual journey. When the Israelites crossed the Jordan, the army consisted of men from all twelve tribes. Together they subdued the land. They were a people of God. While each man retained his tribal identity, they were together in the battles. When the Canaanites were subdued and the land was divided, the Reubenites, Gadites, and half-tribe of Manasseh returned to their allotted territory. They then built a monument to represent the unity of the nation divided by a river. It was a monument visible to the people on both sides of the Jordan.

Discipleship is about a personal relationship with the Lord. It is not, however, an individual sport. We need to be engaged along the way with others. We need the encouragement of others in our struggles. We need to encourage others in their struggles. We learn together by sharing our experiences and insights.

Maturing as a disciple is more than just worshiping together on Sunday, during a midweek Bible study, or at a prayer meeting. Maturing takes meeting together to dig into the Word, sharing needs, and bearing one another's burdens.

Looking In: Are you engaged with a mentor or in a small group? Do you share what the Lord is doing in your life?

Looking Out: Are you mentoring another man or men? Do you set aside time for sharing what the Lord is doing in the lives of your men? Are you engaged in advancing Christ's kingdom together? Are you a band of brothers?

> They devoted themselves to the apostles' teaching and to the fellowship, to the breaking of bread and to prayer. Everyone was filled with awe, and many wonders and miraculous signs were done by the apostles. All the believers were together and had everything in common. Selling their possessions and goods, they gave to anyone as he had need. Every day they continued to meet together in the temple courts. They broke bread in their homes and ate together with glad and sincere hearts, praising God and enjoying the favor of all the people. And the LORD added to their number daily those who were being saved.
>
> —Acts 2:42–47

A disciple advances Christ's kingdom together with other believers.

The Lord Is Peace. Therefore, Be at Rest.

> "… 'The LORD your God is giving you rest and has granted you this land.' … 'until the LORD gives them rest, as he has done for you, and until they too have taken possession of the land that the LORD your God is giving them …"
>
> —Joshua 1:13, 15

> The LORD gave them rest on every side …
>
> —Joshua 21:44

Rest was a physical place. For the children of Israel, it meant not having to wander in the desert. It meant having a place of their own and being where the Lord wanted them. The Lord calls us to a physical place.

Rest is also a spiritual state. Recall earlier comments in this book about rest, describing rest as the guaranteed continuance of hope and the assurance of being with the Lord in eternity. Rest is the personal, deep experience of spiritual peace that comes when we make Jesus the Lord of our lives. It means submission or surrender. It is the abundant, Spirit-filled life.

Finally, rest is an eternal state. When we enter God's rest, we experience His peace in the present life. We have rest in the assurance that we have been saved. There is also the assurance that when this life is over, we will enjoy the presence of the Lord in eternity.

A man was challenged to pray with authority. Before going to bed one night he received an e-mail that upset him. He could not get to sleep because of his anger. He confronted Satan, commanding him, in Jesus' name, to leave. The thought left, but returned in a few minutes. He prayed again and Satan was gone. He slept peacefully through the night.

Looking In: Have you found rest in the Lord? Are you where the Lord wants you to be? Are you doing what He wants you to do? Are there areas of your life in which you are not being obedient, and, as a result, are not receiving His rest?

Looking Out: Are there men in your midst who are not receiving rest? Are you leading them to release control of their lives to the Lord? Are they "yoked" with the Master? Are you encouraging your men to find their calling? Are you helping them to plug into their calling?

> "Come to me, all who labor and are heavy laden, and I will give you rest. Take my yoke upon you, and learn from me, for I am gentle and lowly in heart, and you will find rest for your souls. For my yoke is easy, and my burden is light."
>
> —Matt. 11:28–30

> "Peace I leave with you; my peace I give you. I do not give to you as the world gives."
>
> —John 14:27

> And the peace of God, which transcends all understanding, will guard your hearts and your minds in Christ Jesus.
>
> —Philippians 4:7

A disciple enjoys the peace of the Lord.

For His Name's Sake.

Endnotes

1 The tribe of Manasseh was the largest of the tribes of Israel. Moses allotted one half of the tribe lands east of the Jordan, along with the tribes of Reuben and Gad. The remainder of the tribe of Manasseh received lands on the west side of the river, once the Promised Land had been conquered.

2 R. Laird Harris, Gleason L. Archer, Jr. and Bruce K. Waltke *Theological Wordbook of the Old Testament*, (Chicago: Moody, 1980) Vol. II, #1323, pg. 562–3

3 Brother Lawrence, *Practice the Presence of God*, (Ada, MI: Revell, 1967).

4 Larry Crabb, *Basic Principles of Biblical Counseling*, (Grand Rapids: Zondervan, 1975)

5 To each believer he gives a grace gift (Rom. 12:3–8), encouragement gifts (1 Cor. 12:8–11), and equipping or body gifts (Eph. 4:11–13) To some he gives leadership gifts (1 Cor. 12:27–31).

6 The candy cane reminds us of the meaning of Christmas. The hard white candy represents the virgin birth, the solid rock on which the Church stands, and the firmness of God's promises. The J shape represents Jesus as our savior and the staff of the Good Shepherd. The small red stripes represent Jesus' scourging, while the large red stripe represents Jesus' blood shed on the cross.